A Feast at God's Table

A Feast at God's Table

90 Inviting Articles

SUSAN ROSE

....

ABUNDANCE PRESS

....

Dedication

To all of my supporters:

You are "givers," every single one, with your lives reflecting the transformation of the Lord. All of you know who you are. Your help and encouragement certainly means a lot.

I'm sure the Lord will bless you for freely sowing this seed.

I sincerely thank you.

Contents

Introduction

As you read through this book, I know you will be blessed. And after finishing it, one thing you'll understand is that the Christian faith consists of a close personal relationship between you and God. *Nothing less will do.* If you don't know the Lord intimately, then this devotional writing will certainly show you how.

Our Lord is merciful and good. His heart overflows with grace. The truth we hear at His table is always perfect.

Every Christian is given a unique purpose and a glorious mission—one that is nourished by God. When we partake of what He serves, we're always strengthened for the days ahead.

Almost every one of the 90 articles in this book springs from something God has taught me at work, home, or during travels. Because of this being a devotional book, I've excluded most personal detail so that through the reading, you'll become closer to God and not to me.

All of my articles are dated, but you'll see they are not in chronological order. I've only preserved the dates for the readers' general perspective.

As you read this book, I pray that you'll be encouraged and directed in the particular areas the Lord is pressing hard upon.

I join you in His abundant grace.

Susan Rose

x

You prepare a table before me in the presence of my enemies; you anoint my head with oil; my cup runs over. Surely goodness and mercy shall follow me all the days of my life; and I will dwell in the house of the LORD forever.

Psalm 23:5-6

Faith

Dare to Dream

January 23, 2007

I want my life to count for something of eternal value. I want to be a positive influence on those around me. Do you have these thoughts? Let me assure you, they're coming from God. He's leading you in a quest for significance—a desire that grows while abiding in Him. As Christians, we have the power to walk away from mediocrity. We're called to make a phenomenal impact in this world.

Have you come to a place where you're discovering new hope at nearly every turn? Is the Lord renewing your mind and strengthening your spirit with His truth and love? Then go forth, Christian, and be true to your new vision! Let faith lift you up and show you the glory of the Lord. You'll do the work that Jesus did, and even more!

Most assuredly, I say to you, he who believes in Me, the works that I do he will do also; and greater works than these he will do, because I go to My Father - John 14:12.

Do you want to please God? Then believe Him! Dreams that result from faith in a living word from God are no longer dreams, but reality. Continue spending time with the Lord, allowing Him to teach and transform you. Embrace His hope and purpose for every day. Dare to dream those dreams inspired by the Most High God.

By faith Enoch was taken away so that he did not see death, "and was not found, because God had taken him;" for before he was taken he had this testimony, that he pleased God. But without faith it is impossible to please Him, for he who comes to God must believe that He is, and that He is a rewarder of those who diligently seek Him – Hebrews 11:5-6.

The dreams You plant in us are truly alive! They live and breathe and grow! Thank You, Lord, for these treasures You have given us. May they become as large as Your intentions.

A Paradigm Shift

Faith is the primary path to our destiny, and sooner or later, every Christian comes to a frightening crossroads. We find ourselves with a great and pressing need that squarely meets with our glaring inabilities. At this place, we know we must have God's rescuing hand. Without His favor and grace we will suffer significant loss.

In the past, we trusted God to give us a good parking spot or to help us find clothes on sale. It cost us nothing to trust Him because the stakes weren't very high. But now we are faced with life-changing loss if God doesn't intervene.

We are sovereignly brought to this crossroads only because we are ready to be there. At this point, if we choose to embrace God even more tightly, He will give us greater depths of vision and hope. A paradigm begins to shift. The truth doesn't change, but our level of understanding certainly does. New life springs forth as we faithfully wait upon God.

Now to Him who is able to do exceedingly abundantly above all that we ask or think, according to the power that works in us, to Him be glory in the church by Christ Jesus to all generations, forever and ever. Amen – Ephesians 3:20-21.

Lord, we're so thankful for the precise choreography You apply to our lives. At just the right time, You increase our need of faith. Then we actually have an increase of faith because You feed it with Your Word and Your amazing grace. It's great to be cared for in such unique ways.

The Peace of God

Stress has been defined as "being in a situation where we expect to fail and thereby lose respect and favor." Oh dear! Nobody in their right mind wants to feel this way. Most of us work hard to avoid being "in over our heads." When we have a choice, we pick situations in which we feel comfortable and confident—with just enough challenge to make us look good.

Christians can read about "casting our cares upon the Lord." But when we actually experience the rescuing arm of God from stressors both great and small, we find new confidence in His care for us. Surrendering to His tender, nurturing love is a step of faith that brings a new beginning. We won't find ourselves worried nearly as much or as often. Anxiety fades away as we're transformed to be the calming influences of this turbulent world.

Be anxious for nothing, but in everything by prayer and supplication, with thanksgiving, let your requests be made known to God; and the peace of God, which surpasses all understanding, will guard your hearts and minds through Christ Jesus - Philippians 4:6-7.

Lord, You are so good at removing evil and giving us Your goodness in its place. All we have to do is believe. Receiving Your wonderful peace in place of stress is miraculous!

Obtaining a Good Testimony

June 28, 2015

Now faith is the substance of things hoped for, the evidence of things not seen. For by it the elders obtained a good testimony – Hebrews 11:1-2.

Why must we endure the rigorous testing of our faith? In my own experience, these trials have drawn me closer to the actual Person of God—not simply in a "God, please help me" way, but by pulling me into a place of really knowing and communicating with Him.

As testing continues and as the stakes become higher, I find myself asking, "Can God be trusted?" Can He be relied on to correct me if I've misunderstood His words? And then, when I search for answers to those audacious questions, I am confronted by the heart of God. I hear it beating steadfastly, with the utmost integrity, and with a beautifully intense love that settles all of my uncertainties.

When the Lord gives us a personal promise, and then He requires that we wait a long time for its appearance, we should know that He has good reasons for moving slowly. As I've just described, waiting on God is a season of drawing near to Him. But with our Lord, there is always an abundance of purpose.

While we anticipate the arrival of His promise, God draws us irretrievably into our destiny. At first, we're given the general framework, but the details are withheld. As we continue to wait, we're carefully transformed with a series of tribulations—the kind that last only a day, or maybe even a week. A few will last a month or more. Whatever the duration, these troubling events continue to land on our doorstep for us to deal with, and then they go. With each victory, we see God's glory released—more of His character unveiled for us to marvel at and depend on. Time goes by, and our discernment is sharpened. We're led to hidden reserves of truth. We learn the importance of timing.

While walking with God, He reveals exciting new details of our destiny. Our passion increases for this vision that is exceedingly greater than we first expected.

The Word of God clearly reveals His ways of dealing with man. It displays His willingness to do whatever it takes for us to succeed in bringing His Kingdom to Earth. Let's take a look at three patriarchs whose lives offer a pattern that will inspire us—lives that tell us it's okay to "think big" when God has given us a promise:

Jacob was the second-born of twins. When his mother, Rebekah, turned to God for insight regarding the struggle within her pregnant body, He spoke to her of Jacob's destiny: Jacob's people would be stronger than those of his brother, Esau. Jacob would rule over his brother and over his brother's people (Genesis 25:23). So, after Jacob's birth, Rebekah favored him over his brother and certainly told him of his destiny. God stood by His word, even though Jacob took matters of destiny into his own hands by lying to his father and cheating his brother. God continued being faithful, in spite of Jacob's manipulation and his overconfident attitude. Through a series of trials in which Jacob received a large dose of his own medicine, he was enlightened by God and made fit for his destiny. He had become a humble, Godly leader of a strong people—the father of Joseph and the future nation of Israel.

Joseph received his own promise of success through a dream from God, though I'm sure he had moments of uncertainty. When he was thrown into a pit by his brothers and left to die, he certainly turned to God, crying for help and also for explanation. Things looked better for a while in Potiphar's house, until Joseph was slandered and sent to prison. The Egyptian prison was abhorrent, but Joseph kept his heart aligned with God and rose to a position of trust. Another disappointment came in the form of a final two-year wait, mainly because of God's timing. But Joseph still trusted the Lord and therefore was ready when the big day finally came—the day when Pharaoh called for Joseph's help to interpret his dreams—the day when Joseph was released from prison and promoted to second-in-command of Egypt (Genesis 41:39-41).

David was a mere shepherd boy, chosen by God and anointed by Samuel to be the next King of Israel. David waited many difficult years for his coronation. Through seasons of hardship and persecution, David worshiped the Lord with song and dance, and with psalms inspired by the Spirit. David sinned, and then he repented. Never pretentious, he cried out to God whenever he was afraid. David defeated giants and mighty armies with the power of God upholding him. After years of severe tribulation and extreme warfare, David received his promise. He was crowned as beloved King over all of Israel (2 Samuel: 5).

Our God is still in the business of miracles and still surrounded by glory. But He is *not* a God of shortcuts. Our faith will still be tested. Our hearts will be sorely tried. Like those who went before us, we will be cleaned up and made ready for the important assignments ahead. We will walk in victory, and our "good testimony" will guide the ones who follow.

Dear Lord, we thank You for restraining, humbling, and carefully preparing us. Your tests are difficult, but since they work for our good, we sincerely thank You for them. Please let Your Word lead us out of any present darkness and into Your glorious light. We want to be where You are, doing only what satisfies You.

From Faith to Faith

August 2, 2009

For I am not ashamed of the gospel of Christ, for it is the power of God to salvation for everyone who believes, for the Jew first and also for the Greek. For in it the righteousness of God is revealed from faith to faith; as it is written, "The just shall live by faith" - Romans 1:16-17.

Within the gospel of Christ, we find the power to be born again. When sufficiently embraced, the gospel continues on with its mighty work. It renews our minds and cleanses us from sin so we can enter God's purpose and blessing. The gospel is truly a gift that keeps on giving!

"For in it the righteousness of God is revealed from faith to faith..." How wonderful! God's character and purpose are given to us in small digestible bites. He starts us out with the sweetest types of easily absorbed food. Then He carefully introduces us to a wide variety of vegetables and meat, one at a time as we are ready. From faith to faith, we progress a single meal at a time.

God wants to promote each one of us, but only when we're prepared. It's more important to do it right than to do it fast. Life with the Lord is not a competition, but an opportunity to know, to believe, and to trust Him.

Dear Lord, we thank for taking us step by step, in increments of faith. You teach us slowly and surely. We grow at different rates, at different times, in different areas. You made us all to be different, and we each have a unique part to play in your kingdom. Thank You, Lord, for not stamping us out with a cookie cutter.

Live Like It's True

July 15, 2011

When the Lord first promises to meet a particular need, His word seems alive and absolutely true. We receive His pledge wholeheartedly. But if much time goes by, the enemy takes full advantage of this delay to plant his evil seeds of doubt. Before long, conditions around us may scream that God cannot be trusted. The battle is on! We're torn between what we see and what we know. Our physical perception tells us we may have misunderstood the voice of the Lord. But the Spirit assures us that we heard correctly and that God is not a liar.

The Lord bestows many blessings without requiring us to wait. They come automatically. We might take these blessings for granted or even think we earned them. But certain gifts come only after a season of waiting—sometimes for God's timing, and sometimes because we need to be tested. The promise of their arrival is a tool in God's hand to purify us and enlarge our faith. This cleansing and growth must transpire before any manifest victory.

As we press on to fight for what is ours, strong emotions will be stirred up. We'll be attacked by spirits of anger, depression, fear and many of their ugly cousins. Because God's promises to meet a genuine need of ours, the powers of darkness tempt us to look at a future without that provision. According to them, loneliness, poverty and illness are surely on the road ahead. And this might actually be true if we succumb to negative emotions and take the wrong turn. A growing faith is critical.

Be strong and of good courage; do not be afraid, nor be dismayed, for the LORD your God is with you wherever you go - Joshua 1:9.

Every day is filled with choices. We can choose the high roads of holiness where the voice of God is loud and clear. We can refuse to be afraid, depressed or angry. Choosing rightly, however, doesn't exempt us from walking through dark places, so we must know that God abides in the clouds and in the storms (Nahum 1:3). Then, with eyes of faith, we'll find treasure in this darkness:

I will give you the treasures of darkness and hidden riches of secret places, that you may know that I, the LORD, who call you by your name, am the God of Israel - Isaiah 45:3.

Yes, much is to be gained while waiting on the Lord. Our emotions may waiver, but if we take courage and live each day like His promise is true, then we'll be on course to receive the blessing in its appointed time.

Remember the word to Your servant, upon which You have caused me to hope. This is my comfort in my affliction, for Your word has given me life - Psalm 119:49-50.

Thank You, Lord, for all Your precious promises and for Your many manifest blessings. Thank You for being with us at every step on the road, so we need not be afraid. Please open our eyes so we can find treasure in every darkness. We praise You for causing all things to work together for our good.

Faith is a Spiritual Substance

December 26, 2006

Now faith is the substance of things hoped for, the evidence of things not seen - Hebrews 11:1.

Faith is an actual, spiritual substance. The shape of it often changes, but its existence is solid and real. Being stewards of this incredible gift and the power it contains, we should diligently guard it, work to cultivate its growth and strive to exercise it fully.

- Faith is the fiery touch of God that ignites our hope and kindles our dreams until they blaze into sight.

- Faith is alive. Like a beating heart, it pumps Jesus' blood of victory into every promise.

- Faith is God's seal upon our spirits—His pledge that we'll have what we're waiting for, in His perfect timing.

- Faith is the glue that bonds us tightly to the Lord during those trials that last for years. It keeps us from wiggling loose.

- Faith radically improves our vision. We see proof of God's love everywhere.

- Faith solicits the very best, "even if it hurts." It stirs up the bravest prayers—the kind that touch our Savior's heart.

- Faith is the fuel that propels us forward, day after day, always nearer to the Prize.

God never forces His gifts on us. Even the vital substance of faith is set before us to choose. We can take just a little, or we can load our hearts and minds to overflowing.

We can feast on the written Word and be filled with anticipation. We can listen for the Spirit's encouraging voice and watch for the pictures He paints in our minds. We can welcome God to our dreams at night and receive His presentations. Every type of word from the Lord will feed and increase our faith.

So then faith comes by hearing, and hearing by the word of God - Romans 10:17.

We are so thankful, Lord. You give us beautiful promises and also the faith to believe them. Faith is a gift to be prized as one of Your finest.

The Fullness of His Purpose

March 9, 2006

Every Christian is given a unique purpose and a glorious mission. But in the interest of building our faith, God doesn't provide us with step -by-step plans. Our first instruction may be simple—nothing more than a general direction in which to move.

Sometimes we see a short way ahead as we travel unfamiliar roads. If we don't yet see the form or the color of what God has planned for us, the voice of Hope will whisper of advancement, just around the bend.

The enemy suggests that God is cruel—that He requires entirely too much from us. We're told that our hope is foolish and that God cannot be trusted. But if we listen closely to the Spirit, we are perfectly strengthened for the days ahead.

For I know the thoughts that I think toward you, says the LORD, thoughts of peace and not of evil, to give you a future and a hope - Jeremiah 29:11.

We can always thank the Lord that we're making progress. The fullness of His purpose for us is closer every day. Even if it's actually five or ten years away, it is closer today than the day before. Yes, it is faith that shortens the time and distance. In faith, we lean on God's character, His Word—on all that He is. We know His plans are good. We'll see the richness of His promises at their appointed time.

For the LORD of hosts has purposed, and who will annul it? His hand is stretched out, and who will turn it back? – Isaiah 14:27.

We're so thankful, Lord, for Your perfect plans. You prepare us to walk in Your strategy by transforming us to Your image. The abundance of Your purpose will one day be upon us. What more could we ask?

____

____

____

He Strengthens Hearts

October 2, 2008

Oh, love the LORD, all you His saints! For the LORD preserves the faithful, and fully repays the proud person. Be of good courage, and He shall strengthen your heart, all you who hope in the LORD - Psalm 31:23-24.

When we're full of faith for an important promise from God, then we're energized and glad. We look to the future with joy. But there are times when the enemy subtly convinces us that "it will never happen." Learning to avoid this trickery is critical.

When I first fell for this kind of deception, I was unaware of why I felt so bad. Then I gradually realized that I was suffering from "hope deferred" (Proverbs 13:12). Over time, I've learned to recognize the symptoms when they first begin instead of later when I'm thoroughly depressed. Now I run to God immediately with my doubts and fears. The sooner I do this, the faster He can strengthen my heart.

Christians are often caught in a tug-of-war between faith and hopelessness. When we feel the enemy pulling us into disbelief, we absolutely must resist. Moving toward God through the Word, prayer and worship will always put distance between us and enemy lies.

Thank You, Lord, for preserving us from enemy lies. We will always put our hope in You. Our hearts will be strong as we draw ever closer.

The Integrity of God

June 7, 2009

For all of God's promises have been fulfilled in Christ with a resounding "Yes!" And through Christ, our "Amen" (which means "Yes") ascends to God for his glory – 2 Corinthians 1:20 NLT.

Have you received a personal promise from the Lord—one you've been waiting to see unfold for a very long time? Is the promise so big that at first you had trouble believing it? Is the promise so important (affecting lives that you love) that settling for anything less is unthinkable? To have such a promise is truly a blessing, but the waiting for it to arrive can be difficult. Once we see the glory ahead, it's hard to live in today.

Waiting on the Lord is challenging, especially when the promise is remarkable. But during the delay we learn amazing new things. We find out much about ourselves, and we learn great things about our God. Today, the Spirit reminded me of His integrity. To have integrity means to be honest, true, honorable, admirable, reputable, reliable, authentic, legitimate, genuine, sincere, earnest, serious—and in God's case, I'm sure there's plenty more. With Him, we get the deluxe supernatural version.

Yes, I'm counting on God to keep His promises to me, both big and small. I'm sure He will do it.

Thank You, Lord, for giving us a "heads up" for the months and years ahead. Having a wonderful promise gives us reason to have faith—even "great faith," if we have to wait. And thank You for being the One we can trust when it seems that the world is falling apart.

____

____

____

____

____

Pull the Trigger of Faith

September 17, 2009

We're required to walk through some frightful places here on Earth. We find ourselves in settings where voices scream the most dreadful lies! Clouds of depression try to engulf and paralyze. Thoughts and emotions that seem like our own will come from the enemy to trap us. Being overwhelmed by these negative feelings, we're tempted to submit to evil demands—to discard our hope in God—to give up the fight and go home.

But on the darkest of days, wherever we find ourselves, God wants us to rise above the howling winds of deception and the weariness of oppression. These excursions onto the battleground are part of the Christian experience—part of our ongoing training. We're taught to do this, day by day and step by step. Earth is our training ground.

Difficult times are actually used by the Lord to strengthen our spiritual muscles We get to know God and His truth in new and exciting ways. When we're under attack, the Holy Spirit gives us pertinent truth to match our current dilemma. Then we can pull the powerful trigger of faith and blast away! Like a frightful machine gun, the declaration of God's Word will send the demons running.

So Jesus answered and said to them, "Have faith in God. For assuredly, I say to you, whoever says to this mountain, "Be removed and be cast into the sea," and does not doubt in his heart, but believes that those things he says will be done, he will have whatever he says. Therefore I say to you, whatever things you ask when you pray, believe that you receive them, and you will have them - Mark 11:22-24.

Lord, we thank You for the power of Your Word. If we ask anything accordingly and with faith, it will be done. Your Word is a beautiful diagram of Your heart and of Your will. And as members of Your kingdom, we are Your enforcers.

____

____

In the Flesh or the Spirit?

May 29, 2010

That which is born of the flesh is flesh, and that which is born of the Spirit is spirit - John 3:6.

If we're healthy, growing Christians, we'll engage in one trial after another as long as we live on Earth. Whether dealing with a minor inconvenience or a major tribulation, victory only comes from operating in the Spirit—not in works of the flesh. Leaning not on our own understanding, we trust the Lord in all things (Proverbs 3:5). We're given increasing responsibility as we learn through trials to overcome the world and move "from glory to glory" (2 Corinthians 3:18).

This fundamental precept is learned by most new Christians, but it's often forgotten when we're busily entangled with the world. The Holy Spirit is diligent, however, and reminds us when we're in need. He warns us ahead of time that our flesh will not succeed, and if we fall flat because we didn't listen, then he tells us again so we can learn from our failure.

It is the Spirit who gives life; the flesh profits nothing. The words that I speak to you are spirit, and they are life - John 6:63.

Many of our trials include the need to wait a while for God to act. Impatiently stepping out in the flesh can make things worse. But watching and listening for the Spirit will strengthen our faith and keep us on track for success. The time of delay is filled with learning. As we wait, our character is refined, and we're trained in spiritual warfare. The beauty of God's personality is revealed as we interact with Him and quietly reside in the hope of His promise.

Some trials last for years. The enemy will surely tempt us to throw in the towel. Thoughts of taking the matter into our own hands will come quite often and make perfect sense to our flesh. After all, we might have misunderstood. Maybe it was wishful thinking that God would handle the matter in a certain way. When doubts like this arise, we should quickly turn to God for wisdom and clarification. While waiting in the Spirit, we must often pray for guidance.

Years ago, the Lord spoke to me about "something big." I was very excited, thinking that He would move right away to open a door of blessing. When the blessing didn't arrive as I expected, I chose to draw closer to the Lord instead of allowing a wedge to come between us. (Yes, waiting can be a test or a trial.) In answer to my prayer, He has spoken numerous encouraging words to me regarding what I'm waiting for. Many times He's confirmed that I did not misunderstand Him.   Just a few weeks ago He asked that I "submit to His timing."

Much growth and blessing will happen during our trials, as long as we abide in the Lord. Submitting isn't always easy, but being rightly aligned with Him and His purpose brings peace and strength for the days ahead.

Finally, my brethren, be strong in the Lord and in the power of His might. Put on the whole armor of God, that you may be able to stand against the wiles of the devil - Ephesians 6:10-11.

Having faith in You, Lord, is what it takes to overcome works of the flesh. Once again we find the value in this holy endeavor of trusting You.

____

____

____

____

____

____

____

____

____

Feed on His Faithfulness

August 10, 2013

Trust in the LORD, and do good; dwell in the land, and feed on His faithfulness. Delight yourself also in the LORD, and He shall give you the desires of your heart. Commit your way to the LORD, trust also in Him, and He shall bring it to pass – Psalm 37: 3-5.

God has a way of making promises that only He can keep. He "hooks us" with His whispers of miraculous change. He tells us to prepare for new things ahead and also to patiently wait for His perfect timing. With very high hopes, we wait, and wait, and wait some more.

When "tested by waiting," we eventually find ourselves wondering if God will do what we think we heard Him say. When this happens, it's very important to stir up our faith. As we move through our day, "dwelling in the land," we must stay close to the Lord and "feed on His faithfulness." This attribute of God—faithfulness—has amazing powers of renewal.

In my own life, the Lord has always been faithful to answer my prayers for direction. He also keeps me close and well-fed on who He is:

- The personal words of the Spirit, whether fleeting impressions or loud and clear guidance, are precious to me. Whenever I feel faint or lost, I listen for God. If I don't hear His voice, then I pull out my journal and find my bearings in the midst of His previous words to me regarding the promise.

- God's written Word revives a Christian's hope. Because "the Word is God" (John 1:1), it will never fail us. The Word resounds with incredible stories of "great and mighty things" (Jeremiah 33:3), conceived by love within God's heart. The stories, precepts, and revelation all reflect what God intends to do again—for those who will believe.

- Our personal experience with God is an excellent source of encouragement. Taking time to remember past blessings and how they unfolded is always a good idea.

Yes, let us delight ourselves in the Lord—in His faithfulness and all that He is! Let's abide in His generous love and rest in his power. We'll find the brightest hope and the answer to every need.

Dear Lord, You are the bread of life, always ready to feed us with Your presence (John 6:35). Thank You for the revival that comes when we meditate on Your goodness. Your gifts and promises are wonderful, but You Yourself are amazing!

God Wants to Bless Us

April 20, 2014

Therefore I...do not cease to give thanks for you, making mention of you in my prayers...that you may know what is the hope of His calling, what are the riches of the glory of His inheritance in the saints, and what is the exceeding greatness of His power toward us who believe, according to the working of His mighty power which He worked in Christ when He raised Him from the dead and seated Him at His right hand in the heavenly places... - Ephesians 1:15-20.

Some Christians have trouble believing God wants to bless them personally, here on Earth, in practical Earthly ways. They can more easily believe in their salvation from sin and their home in Heaven because this seems far in the future. But if these Christians are required to believe for healing, financial provision, or other blessings that are tangible, then they're intimidated by the necessity of its manifestation. (Weak faith works best in hypothetical or "future" situations.) If God's help doesn't arrive after early prayers or attempts at warfare, these Christians will often make excuses and give up altogether, deciding that it wasn't God's will to help them.

But sometimes our need is so great that we dare not quit. And then, if we're compelled to wait for longer than first anticipated, we're in a perfect position to see God's glory. Our faith will be profoundly tested, but walking closely with the Lord will cause it to grow. Now we can move to higher levels of trust and belief, and God is delighted. However, this prompts the enemy to regroup and pull out more sophisticated weapons, with the goal of inciting fear. Being subject to the rollercoaster of human emotion, our occasional departures from the "high places" can be frightening. Because we abide in a lofty place of faith, the plunge of doubt is now a lot steeper. Such is life for the believer who waits on the Lord for an extended length of time.

Learning to overcome our negative emotions is vital. Life with God is not for the faint of heart. We must take His hand and hold on tight, no matter what.

Our longings for peace, rest, wholeness, love, prosperity and purpose were placed in us by God before we were born. Our wants and needs are stepping stones that lead us deeper into the fragrant garden of His love.

I have come to my garden, my sister, my spouse; I have gathered my myrrh with my spice; I have eaten my honeycomb with my honey; I have drunk my wine with my milk – Song of Solomon 5:1.

Thank You, Lord Jesus, for the gift of Your life. Help us to be in tune with Your holy presence and to treasure every moment with You. Please teach us how to receive Your many other blessings so we can fulfill our purpose in Your Kingdom. Please give us peace while we wait for Your glorious help to arrive.

By all means, ASK!

June 26, 2017

Knowing the heart of God through His written Word helps us recognize demonic lies that try to infiltrate and subvert His truth. The Spirit of God will wave red flags that warn of error. He implores us to beware. The church is always a prime target for enemy lies. For example, a few weeks ago I was in a meeting when the following familiar words came forth: *"Seek God's face and not His hand."* Verbal assent and nods of approval came forth upon this statement, but my hand was soon in the air. I could not let this pass. I respectfully spoke to the group about the error of this teaching.

First of all, "Seek God's face and not His hand" is NOT scripture. I've found it nowhere in the Bible.

I Googled the words "scripture seek God's face not His hand." I found many commentaries that actually support this error—one by a well-known and beloved Christian teacher. I read some of these articles to see if I was missing something important. What I found was a repeated misuse of scripture. The authors all quoted scripture such as Psalm 27:4, Psalm 27:8, 2 Chronicles 7:14, and more. These verses clearly say we should seek God's face. But then these authors *add* the false teaching that we should not seek God's hand—and they don't support this with scripture because it does not exist.

This bogus teaching has been circulating in the church for at least 20 years and probably more, but the words obviously are not from God. An often-used phrase can sound like scripture, especially when it's riding piggy-back on authentic scripture. Many are convinced the words are truth because of their familiarity, and sometimes because of who has spoken them. Christians who are being influenced by a religious spirit are most likely to accept these words that sound so pious.

Along with knowing God's Word, personal experience with His heart is an excellent guide to truth. My time with God has revealed that He is amazingly generous. Jesus' extravagant gift of His life on the cross is enough to prove that point forever. But the Lord continues on, directing us to ask expectantly for what we need. He is eagerly waiting to bless us with provision, healing, peace, power, revelation, and so much more.

And whatever you ask in My name, that I will do, that the Father may be glorified in the Son. If you ask anything in My name, I will do it – John 14:13-14. Jesus could not have made it clearer.

ASK, and it will be given to you; SEEK, and you will find; KNOCK, and it will be opened to you – Matthew 7:7 (capitals are mine). Amen! Lord, we thank You for these invitations adjoined to promises!

I will close with this question: What about prayer? It is an uncontested element of the Christian faith. A major component of prayer is actually "seeking God's hand." Petition and intercession are forms of *asking*. When evil religious spirits tell us to seek God's face but not His hand, their ploy is to shut down our authority and make our prayer ineffective. *They want to stop God's will.*

Be anxious for nothing, but in everything by prayer and supplication, with thanksgiving, let your requests be made known to God; and the peace of God, which surpasses all understanding, will guard your hearts and minds through Christ Jesus – Philippians 4:6-7. Oh, what a glorious promise!

God says that we don't have because we don't ask (James 4:2), so instead of looking to the world, let's always turn to the Lord who is waiting to rain His blessing upon us. Let's confidently pray according to His will and watch His floodgates open. Most of us need God's favor—along with a miracle or two—so let's approach the throne of grace where miracles are born.

We thank You, Lord for Your unchanging truth. Thank You for giving us Your Word and revealing Your bountiful, compassionate heart. Sweet Holy Spirit, we praise Your persistent guidance. Thank You for exposing the strongholds of deception. And thank You especially for welcoming our prayers—the petition and intercession that You have inspired.

The Test of Waiting

August 27, 2017

Passing through the Valley of Weeping (Baca), they make it a place of springs; the early rain also fills [the pools] with blessings - Psalm 84:6 AMPC.

Our time in the "Valley of Baca" is a time of weeping and waiting. In this place of tears, we wait for change. We wait for restoration of what has been lost or stolen. If we submit to the hand of God during this season, then we are supernaturally transformed. Even the barren places around us are watered by His presence.

From a very early age, the enemy began stealing what was mine. Satan meant this theft to cause great harm, but my sovereign God is working to use the terrible loss for good by turning it around, completely and radically. Many will see the final restoration and know that God is good. They will see that He blesses His beloved and includes them in His purpose (Genesis 50:20). When We are weak, then God is strong!

So I will restore to you the years that the swarming locust has eaten, the crawling locust, the consuming locust, and the chewing locust, My great army which I sent among you. You shall eat in plenty and be satisfied, and praise the name of the LORD your God, who has dealt wondrously with you; and My people shall never be put to shame. Then you shall know that I am in the midst of Israel: I am the LORD your God and there is no other. My people shall never be put to shame – Joel 2:25-27.

I feel blessed because of my relationship with the Lord. I believe that all of His many promises will manifest in my life and for those in my domain. God has made some personal promises to me that are truly "off the charts."

Kingdom assignments will flourish. One of these remarkable promises was given to me over a decade ago. The waiting has not been easy, as you already know if you've waited a long time for something that is exceptional.

Because of the bright hope God has given me for my future, I sometimes feel like Joseph. He waited as a slave and a prisoner for 13 years before he was elevated to the position foreshadowed in his dreams. I also identify with David, who engaged in many conflicts while waiting for God's time of promotion. The enemy didn't want David on the throne. I feel a kinship with Abraham, who waited 25 years before God's promise of having a child would come to pass. (I don't tell people exactly what God has promised me because its outrageous nature would send contempt my way, as in the cases of Joseph, David, and Abraham.) God sent these men ahead of us, in their obvious human frailty, to shine a light on the tremendous value of waiting for Him to act—on the value of *believing* His "great and mighty" promises (Jeremiah 33:3). God worked miracles through the patriarchs, and He will do the same through us if we persevere in faith.

If God has given you a magnificent promise, you have probably struggled for a while just to believe it. Once you've overcome your initial shock and disbelief—when you learn that it's not about you, but all about God and His plans—you begin the struggle of waiting. If your promise is too good to believe apart from a miracle, then you enter a period of revelation about who God is. A glorious promise from God may be a time of testing—not by fire but by *waiting.*

Behold, I am doing a new thing; now it springs forth, do you not perceive it? I will make a way in the wilderness and rivers in the desert. The wild beasts will honor me, the jackals and the ostriches, for I give water in the wilderness, rivers in the desert, to give drink to my chosen people... - Isaiah 43:19-20 ESV.

While we wait for our "new thing"—the brilliance and excitement of tomorrow—we *must* have help from God. It is He who "makes our way" in the wilderness of waiting. Let's always be thankful for the rivers of provision that flow through our desert of today

Dear Lord, I thank You for dealing wondrously with all of us, from beginning to end.

Intangible Treasure

March 31, 2018

In recent months, I've found myself thanking God repeatedly for the hope He's given to me. This has led me to think of other dynamic, intangible gifts that God has been generous with. Let's take a look at the unseen treasures of faith, courage, and hope.

FAITH – Now faith is the substance of things hoped for, the evidence of things not seen. For by it the elders obtained a good testimony. By faith we understand that the worlds were framed by the word of God, so that the things which are seen were not made of things which are visible – Hebrews 11:1-3.

It all begins when we're saved by faith (Ephesians 2:8). Then we "hear through the word of Christ" (Romans 10:17), and faith begins to grow.

- Faith is a multi-faceted marvel, and it's called by many names: trust, belief, and confidence, to name a few.

- Faith begins small but arrives on the scene with much excitement. Sometimes the exuberance gets it wedged in tight places, but these challenges help it mature.

- The frustration, discontent, and pain of this world are all good fuels that put faith in a higher gear. Earth is a training ground where we grow from "faith to faith" (Romans 1:17) and thereby from "glory to glory" (2 Corinthians 3:18).

- The main source of our faith is the Word of God. The Word *is* God (John 1:1), so our foundation is rock solid. The Word is our rock, our fortress, and our deliverer (2 Samuel 22:2).

Even with a mile-long list of bullet points, faith must be tested to come fully alive. To move through its strange and beautiful passageways, we're asked to lay down our life as we've known it thus far. Leaving our comfort zone far behind, faith requires that we submit unreservedly to God's Word. When snarling "giants of the land" lurch at us from the shadows, we learn to slay them with a gleaming sword of Truth. When at times we feel the ground shake, we'll run to our Rock to hold on tight—to Him and His comforting words. The invisible, untouchable treasure of faith remains "intangible," but its value to us is growing exponentially. Obviously, faith has a learning curve that is often harsh and steep, but this vibrant realm is where transformation and healing abide.

COURAGE – Have I not commanded you? Be strong and of good courage; do not be afraid, nor be dismayed, for the LORD your God is with you wherever you go – Joshua 1:9.

Faith begets courage. I believe it's a package deal. This "deal" is only possible because God is our Foundation. When we believe a particular Word of the Lord, we're enabled to step boldly in that direction—though we always have a *choice*. (God commands us to be brave, but He doesn't force us.) With every courageous step, we're strengthened even more because we see the power of the Word at work—released by our obedience.

In the midst of a trial, we may not think about courage. Most often we're praying for more faith, and we're asking God to be strong on our behalf. But personal courage is a requirement that shadows faith. It's a vital response to the challenges we face. If we find it running low, we simply need to ask for more.

HOPE – Return to the stronghold, you prisoners of hope. Even today I declare that I will restore double to you – Zechariah 9:12.

Just like faith, our hope rests squarely on God's Word and on His character. Hope in the goodness of God inspires vision for the future. Dreams from the heart of the Lord are conceived within *us* because of a hopeful environment. But even when hope is dashed to bits on the sharp rocks of testing, it will become whole again if it's based on Truth and revived with courage. Just a fragment of hope can pull you back into the peaceful province where high expectations reign.

Hope may be unseen—fully concealed from untrained eyes. But it is mighty and relentless. It will hold us captive for a lifetime if that is required.

We thank You, Lord, for blessing us with faith, courage, hope, and other intangible wealth. Victory flows freely through these divine channels. You have equipped us with excellence.

HOPE

Got Hope?

While I was driving home from work one day, the Holy Spirit spoke to me about hope. I was feeling thankful that I *have* hope, and I was praising God for this. Then I noticed a bumper sticker in the traffic lane to my right. A spin-off of the cute "Got milk?" advertisement, this sticker said "Got hope?' I was driving on I-75 at 70 miles per hour, so noticing the bumper sticker wasn't a trivial thing. *I'm sure the Spirit made me look.* I know that God was emphasizing the value of hope, and this humorous interaction with Him brought laughter to my praise.

The Apostle Paul wrote powerful words about hope:

To them God willed to make known what are the riches of the glory of this mystery among the Gentiles: which is Christ in you, the hope of glory - Colossians 1:27.

If we have Jesus, then we have HOPE! This hope is for more than "just getting by." We have hope for *glory*—big, fat, miraculous glory that only God can deliver! A different but valid twist on this scripture is: With Christ abiding in us, then our Father has hope for all the amazing glory He has planned!

Abiding in Christ is a glorious arrangement! Thank You, Lord, for giving us such great hope. And thank You for the hope You take in Jesus dwelling within us. With Him, we can do all things.

When Hope Arrives

November 17, 2013

Now may the God of hope fill you with all joy and peace in believing, that you may abound in hope by the power of the Holy Spirit – Romans 15:13.

If God has a middle name, I believe it might be "Hope." The Greek word for hope is "Elpis," pronounced "el-peace'." This means "to anticipate and welcome properly." It is "the expectation of what is certain" (Strong's 1680).

Return to the stronghold, you prisoners of hope. Even today I declare that I will restore double to you – Zechariah 9:12.

Let us always be prisoners of hope. Let's pursue God and His glory until we prevail!

A few days ago, something dear to me was under attack. I felt overwhelmed, and I found myself sinking into a thick mire of oppression. I called out to God for help. I told Him I was weak, wounded, and desperately in need of His strength. "If I'm to go on, I must have more of You, Lord," is what I repeatedly said. Within 24 hours of this prayer, the powerful presence of hope arrived. It came on the wings of revelation, and it pulled me from the bog of my despair.

This remarkable rescue from the torment of enemy lies has me praising the attribute of God called hope. I want to share some thoughts that are rising up within me:

- Because hope literally carries the power of God, it breathes life into "dying" situations. The strength it imparts is very real, and its impact is eternal.

- Reaching directly from the heart of the Lord, hope wipes away our tears, heals our wounded hearts, restores our fading sight, and removes the layer of dust from our future.

- Hope arrives bearing gifts. Among them are lightness, peace, joy, courage and strength.

- Only the Spirit and the Word can build the framework of a strong hope that endures through lengthy trials.

- Hope is a beloved brother of "Faith." These mighty warriors march with us into battle and onward to our place of triumph.

Thank You, Lord, for being our "Hope of glory" (Colossians 1:27). Because of You, the enemy can never quench the flame of expectation that burns within us. Because of You, our lives are bright with vision.

God Repeats Himself

February 27, 2006

I've been taught that when God repeats Himself, then we should really pay attention. A few years ago, I found some verses that are repeated almost word for word—three times! Let's take a close look, and let's believe what God is showing us through the words of a psalmist:

Why are you cast down, O my soul? And why are you disquieted within me? Hope in God, for I shall yet praise Him for the help of His countenance - Psalm 42:5.

Why are you cast down, O my soul? And why are you disquieted within me? Hope in God; for I shall yet praise Him, the help of my countenance and my God - Psalm 42:11.

Why are you cast down, O my soul? And why are you disquieted within me? Hope in God; for I shall yet praise Him, the help of my countenance and my God - Psalm 43:5.

The full content of Psalms 42 and 43 explains why the psalmist writes these words. Just like us, his faith was being tested. When he became discouraged, he would remember his past experience with God. He would think of all the times he was helped and protected. Memories of God's help to others would also come to mind. The psalmist prophesied by writing the words. He then set his hope on God helping him again.

Just as the psalmist did, we should do also.

Dear Lord, Your Word is full of examples for us to follow. Thank You for shining Your light on this one. Thank You for repeating it three times!

God Is an Encourager

September 20, 2012

Why are you cast down, O my soul? And why are you disquieted within me? Hope in God, for I shall yet praise Him for the help of His countenance - Psalm 42:5.

I wrote about Psalm 42:5 in 2006. Now six years later, I'm writing again. I'm very much impressed that God has repeated these words almost exactly in Psalm 42:11 and 43:5. By the pen of a psalmist, the Spirit urges us repeatedly to put our hope in God. Because God states His message three times, I know He means business. A triple dose of hope and power can be received if we will hear and believe.

God is an encourager. His words are a call to hang in there and don't give up because His help is on the way. We're told to wait expectantly for *Him* because He is the answer. His love, His grace, His mercy, His power—these saving attributes are part of who He is.

In a couple areas that I pray for, I've come to a place of desperation. But this is good desperation—the kind that makes me totally dependent on God. Throughout the day, I've found myself repeating the scripture above. Sometimes I entreat the Lord—*My hope is in You. I need Your help*. Other times I announce my Hope in God with confidence and joy, knowing that He has inspired me to proclaim His powerful Word.

Yes! Put your hope in the Lord, and wait on Him! He is the One who will not disappoint.

Blessed is the man who trusts in the LORD, whose trust is the LORD. He is like a tree planted by water, that sends out its roots by the stream, and does not fear when heat comes, for its leaves remain green, and is not anxious in the year of drought, for it does not cease to bear fruit – Jeremiah 17:7-8 ESV.

Thank You, Lord, for Your precious gift of hope. I can't imagine life without hope in You. This hope aligns with courage and joy because YOU are the answer to our need. Thank You for all the promises we look forward to, and thank You for being perfectly faithful to Your Word.

# Rest in Hope

February 11, 2006

I have set the LORD always before me. Because He is at my right hand I shall not be moved. Therefore my heart is glad, and my glory rejoices. My flesh also will rest in hope - Psalm 16:8-9.

Hope in God feels cool and fresh like the mist of early morning.

It offers shade, like a large, leafy tree.

It shines a light in the darkest of storms.

It is mighty but speaks with a gentle voice.

It is the living breath of God touching your cheek.

Don't ever ignore God's sweet voice of Hope when He speaks to your discouraged soul. When you feel His loving caress on your weary shoulders, you should stop to let it nurture and refresh you.

Rest in Hope, and let it help you through every trial.

Lord, You are always our wonderful Hope. You assure us that all is well, and Your faithfulness is the icing on the cake.

LOVE

Handle With Care

February 18, 2006

A father sat in his recliner, reading the Saturday news and drinking coffee. One of his young sons played on the floor nearby. This man watched his child, and his heart swelled with love. After a while, the father began to wonder what his other son was doing. He said, "Sammy, will you please go find Luke? Tell him to come inside for a minute." Sammy ran to the fenced back yard and saw his brother playing under a large shade tree.

With a shrill voice, he yelled, "Hey, Luke! Daddy says to get in the house right now! He wants to talk to you!" To Luke's four-year-old ears, the message was foreboding. It seemed that he was in trouble, but he didn't know what for. Confused and sad, Luke hid behind the tree and quietly cried until his father came to find him.

Sammy misrepresented his father by conveying the message poorly. His choice of words and tone of voice drastically altered the meaning and caused his brother to be afraid.

Even adults fall prey to careless or unkind communication. Damage is done, and lives are changed by imprudent verbal mistakes, often delivered from prideful lips. An effective messenger always delivers the words exactly as they are intended, not filtering them through personal views or emotions.

For Christians—ambassadors of Christ—the standard is very high. While speaking as friends, neighbors, teachers, preachers, and prophets, we must handle truth with the utmost care. Our words should align with God's heart Truth must always be spoken with love.

Mercy and truth have met together; Righteousness and peace have kissed - Psalm 85:10.

Dear Father, we're so thankful for Your tender, patient love for us. You sometimes correct us, but Your words are never condemning. Your love always lifts us high and moves us forward. Your Word sets a clear and beautiful standard for us to follow. Please fill our hearts each day with kindness and love for those around us.

Loving Our Enemies

Learning to love our enemies is difficult, and that's an understatement. Emotional challenges and ethical questions arise. When does a simple offense cross the line and become abuse? What do we stand up to, and what do we let slide?

How we respond is important. If a person is being abusive, we should calmly and respectfully stand up for what is right. We should never enable sin by condoning it. Sometimes "tough love" is required. The most loving action may be one of discipline. Of course, turning the other cheek is most often called for, but this mild response can be difficult.

All situations are different, so there is no well-defined blueprint for success. However, some basic requirements exist for loving our enemies effectively:

- <u>Abide in Christ</u>. Loving the enemy is not possible apart from unity with our Lord. We can't bear good fruit unless we abide in the Vine (John 15:4).

- <u>Humility is essential</u>. A willingness to submit ourselves to God at every turn is required. Humility pleases God tremendously, so we gain much more from Him than we ever give up to a human being (1 Peter 5:6,7).

- <u>Suffering is required if we're going to be Christ-like</u>. We learn the "fellowship of his suffering" (Philippians 3:10) at the hands of our enemies. Even those who love us will occasionally hurt us, so we shouldn't be surprised by the actions of those who don't.

- <u>Don't hold on to anger</u>. Prolonged anger is destructive, but the prayer of a wounded Christian for their assailant truly blesses the heart of God and gets Him involved.

- <u>We must not condemn</u>. Each time we're injured or oppressed, we have an opportunity to pray for the offender. With new insight into their darkness, we can intercede effectively. If we chcose prayer instead of anger, then life-changing power is released to the situation.

- <u>Forgiveness is a hallmark of Jesus' teaching</u>. He forgave us completely and paid for our sin with His blood. He requires that we forgive others. Anything less is unacceptable.

Therefore be merciful, just as your Father also is merciful. Judge not, and you shall not be judged. Condemn not, and you shall not be condemned. Forgive, and you will be forgiven - Luke 6:36-37.

Lord, we thank You for loving us when we were still "the enemy." Your blood washed us clean and transformed our hearts, so it can also wash those who mistreat us. When our emotions get in the way of Your purpose, let Your love rise up within us and win the victory.

Loving or Critical?

March 25, 2011

Christians can easily fall into the trap of being critical. Some of us are already in the habit of labeling behavior as "right, wrong, or questionable." Our personality may predispose us to being analytical or opinionated. If we let the enemy exploit these tendencies, then we'll be led down a dangerous path where our thoughts become overly critical, and we mistakenly think we've gained maturity and discernment.

Unless we no longer listen, God's Spirit will sound an alarm. He will make us aware of the fork in our road ahead. To the right is the road of love and intercession. To the left is a busy freeway taken by angry Christians who respond to the world with bitterness and judgement.

Spirit-filled Christians choose the road of love and intercession. Their Godly discernment leads them to act and pray effectively when encountering unholy behavior from those in their realm of influence. The spirits of "self-righteousness" and "pride" don't ever choose this route. Neither do "offense" and "indignation." Those aligned with these unholy spirits will take the crowded thoroughfare where they will criticize with others of like mind.

Being hurt or annoyed by someone's sinful conduct is no excuse for putting up cold, hard walls of protection Christians are not allowed to take offense and be angry. Our job is to forgive the sinner and pray for them. Not just once or twice, but "seventy times seven."

Then Peter came to Him and said, "Lord, how often shall my brother sin against me, and I forgive him? Up to seven times?" Jesus said to him, "I do not say to you, up to seven times, but up to seventy times seven - Matthew 18:21-22.

If we want to be useful in the kingdom of God, we must always choose to love. This includes humbling ourselves and becoming a living sacrifice—just as Jesus did for us. We can't demand the best treatment every minute of the day. Instead, we must look for ways to serve.

...love your enemies, bless those who curse you, do good to those who hate you, and pray for those who spitefully use you and persecute you, that you may be sons of your Father in heaven; for He makes His sun rise on the evil and on the good, and sends rain on the just and on the unjust - Matthew 5:43-45.

Thank You, Lord, for showing us the way. Your example of humility and love is woven throughout the gospel with beautiful crimson thread. Please keep our thoughts and words aligned with Your purpose. Keep our feet on the "highway of holiness" (Isaiah 35:8) where Your purpose is reached through mercy and grace.

Reciprocal Love

February 20, 2012

Because he has set his love upon Me, therefore I will deliver him; I will set him on high, because he has known My name. He shall call upon Me, and I will answer him; I will be with him in trouble; I will deliver him and honor him. With long life I will satisfy him, and show him My salvation. - Psalm 91:14-16.

This is my desire—to set my love upon the Lord and to know His name. What I receive in return, right here on Earth, is amazing. Grace incarnate greets me every day.

God values our love for Him so highly that He reciprocates as no human being can: He answers when we call. He's with us in every trouble. He honors us. He delivers us and sets us on high. He satisfies us with long life. He shows us His continuous salvation.

All of this is ours, just for loving the Lord!

How we respond to God's wondrous love is important, especially since our old way of doing things has passed away and "All things are new" (2 Corinthians 5:17). In God's kingdom, we are loved so that we may love others. We're blessed so that we may bless others. With God's love and blessing comes the responsibility to "pass it on."

As we are delivered and set on high, the Spirit bids us to help pull others up to our place of safety. Because God answers when we call, the Spirit leads us to pray persistently for others.

Dear Lord, we know that our love for You only exists because You loved us first. But You still respond so graciously when we reflect this love back to You. Your love sets a holy standard for us to embody as we interact with the world—for those who don't yet know Your name.

____

____

Tender Mercies

October 17, 2017

**Do not withhold Your tender mercies from me, O LORD; let Your lovingkindness and Your truth continually preserve me –
Psalm 40:11.**

In recent months, I've been seeing more and more of the tender heart of God. Of course He's always been kind to me. I've not been oblivious to it. But now it seems that a brilliant spotlight is aimed directly at His kindness. The Lord is entirely good, and I view His compassion as simply a part of that. It's the part of Him that cares for our emotions; nurturing, protecting, and healing them. God's tender mercies assure us that we're treasured and safe. They reflect His love in a personal way.

As an example, God recently spoke into my spirit, *"Susan, you don't have to accept these things."* He was referring to some physical ailments that people over 50 assume they have to put up with. He was nudging me toward supernatural healing, and I was very willing to go that way. A few weeks later, a friend just happened to mention the name of Rodney Howard-Browne, a prominent Christian healer in Tampa, Florida. A fire was kindled within me, and I knew I must drive from central Georgia to Tampa. Within days, I had been healed of a long-standing ailment: Due to a hip-replacement surgery in 2009, my left leg was a half inch longer than the right. After nearly eight years of expensive shoe alterations (or hobbling around unevenly), I drove home with legs the exact same length! Jesus had touched me with His mercy! I still get tickled whenever I think of this miracle!

About a month after my healing, it was time for my yearly timeshare vacation in Southwest Florida. I always look forward to this, but now I was feeling uneasy about leaving my cat alone for a week. Foxy is feral, and I'm the only person he doesn't run from. During the past year, Foxy has become emotionally attached to me, and he's happiest when I'm nearby. My concern was that my lengthy absence would make him think he'd been abandoned. I prayed about the situation, and I turned Foxy's welfare over to God. Before I departed, I put out plenty of dry food and water. The cat door was open, so Foxy could come and go as he pleased.

My vacation was cut two days short by Hurricane Irma, and I looked forward to cheering up Foxy with my return. But my little friend was nowhere around. A friend had scared Foxy while watering my newly planted trees. This person reported seeing him flee into the woods just the evening before. I went to bed that night, praying that Foxy would return at any time. But he didn't. Not even for breakfast—his favorite meal.

I've always felt I could bear the loss of Foxy if I knew he hadn't suffered. But the thought of him running away and being gone forever because he thought I had abandoned him—well this would be too much for me. I had grown to love this beautiful, rambunctious creature. He was my friend, and the anguish of not knowing where he was, if he was alive, or how he died would simply be unbearable. (If you've ever loved an animal, then you will understand.)

My next-door neighbor's dirt driveway winds through 17 acres of wooded land. I walked the length of it, calling Foxy's name at least a hundred times, but I got no response. I returned home to eat lunch. I finally asked God to reveal where Foxy was. Right away, He showed me a unique section of woods that lay in the path of where I had already searched. I started out again, repeating my walk on the neighbor's driveway, calling Foxy and talking to him.

God's directions were good, and Foxy came out from his hiding place! Once again, the compassion of the Lord had come to my aid in a glorious way. He loves me, and He knew how I felt about Foxy disappearing. I know He cares for this special cat that He created, and His heart intervened to get Foxy home again. *Dear Lord, I will remember this kindness forever!*

I could cite several more recent occasions of God's mercy and favor toward me, but then this article would be too long. Right now I just want to say, "*Thank You, Lord. You are so good, and I will love You always.*"

This new focus on the Lord's kindness helps me to look past the nagging troubles of today and see the certain blessings of tomorrow. With heightened awareness of the tenderness in God's heart, I'm not afraid to trust Him with my future. So much goodness lies ahead, and I await His promises with gladness.

Jesus, the Anointed One, is always the same—yesterday, today, and forever – Hebrews 13:8 TPT.

Our holy, faithful God, we thank You for never changing. We love Your dependability. And we also love Your relentless works of compassion. They are priceless. Among them are the numerous times You've lifted us up with Your Word. The sweetness of Your truth never fails to be amazing. Please help us to bless YOU by drawing near with sincere praise and worship. We want to enjoy Your presence and be inspired by Your beautiful heart.

A Christ-Like Response

March 25, 2012

When men revile us [wound us with an accursed sting], we bless them. When we are persecuted, we take it patiently and endure it. When we are slandered and defamed, we [try to] answer softly and bring comfort - 1 Corinthians 4:12-13 AMPC.

Many of us have been wrongly programmed to expect fair treatment from others. Even if our Christian growth has undone that expectation, we may still believe that people should treat us well if we present all the facts—if we reason with them in a skillful manner about the issue at hand. But the truth is, if we belong to God, He is teaching us to humbly submit to Him in all things. Our submission is ultimately to the Lord, not to man.

For to you it has been granted on behalf of Christ, not only to believe in Him, but also to suffer for His sake - Philippians 1:29.

Jesus wasn't treated fairly, but He responded to the hatred by giving His life. His pure and holy love is our example. For us, this doesn't come naturally, and it certainly doesn't happen overnight. Our conformation to the image of Christ happens gradually as we're given opportunities to love the ones who mistreat us. These opportunities aren't pleasant, but they're valuable. If we submit to the hand of God, we'll learn much about ourselves and even more about Him:

- Spiritual maturity doesn't make us immune to emotional pain. Instead, it requires that we respond properly in the midst of our pain.

- We can't love the sinful people around us, but "Christ in us" can. Unfairness or unkindness forces us to face this fact and draw upon God to succeed in loving others.

- We can't "win" when the Lord is teaching us to be humble. We must simply submit to Him, trusting that His purpose is met by our gentle response.

- Gcd's purpose doesn't always align with our desire.

- We can learn from our failures. Don't let the enemy tell you otherwise.

But I say to you, love your enemies, bless those who curse you, do good to those who hate you, and pray for those who spitefully use you and persecute you, that you may be sons of your Father in heaven... - Matthew 5:44-45.

The act of prayer is an unseen but beautiful expression of love. This can be our immediate response to being mistreated—one that releases the power of God. We can pray for someone even before our anger and pain subside. (Prayer helps to put our focus on God's purpose. It will curtail our misery and get us back on track emotionally.) But we must pray unselfishly, laying aside our own desire to be held in high esteem. The familiar phrase, "Hurting people hurt people," is something to keep in mind as we intercede for those who are unkind.

Thank You, Lord, for conforming us to Your loving image—no matter how painful the process is. Keep us aware of the honor that comes with each chance to be humble and to love. Help us to pray purely and effectively. We want to please You, Lord, with our responses.

____

____

____

____

____

____

____

The Heart of God

May 26, 2013

If we're going to make a difference in this world, we need to begin at our own front door. Our private, personal behavior needs to be holy, and this includes our thoughts. Our homes must be spiritually clean. If parental guidance is needed with certain material, then why not throw it out completely? Our relationships should be healthy, and agape love should reign.

We must know God's will and pray for the grace to follow it daily. Faithfully reading the Word will keep us in the loop and empowered to succeed.

Knowing the heart of God is vital, and this privilege requires plenty of private time with Him. Of course, an occasional stumble in our Christian walk will certainly happen. But if our plan is to merely "follow enough of the rules" so we can think of ourselves as being good, then we have missed the boat altogether.

Remember: The Pharisees kept the letter of God's law. They followed all of His rules, and they taught others to do the same. *Then they nailed God to a cross.*

Merely following the rules set the Pharisees on a road that led to hell. Obviously, we must do better. Following the rules is good as long as it's done in pursuit of God Himself. We must humbly seek the heart of God that lies *within* His rules.

Though I speak with the tongues of men and of angels, but have not love, I have become sounding brass or a clanging cymbal. And though I have the gift of prophecy, and understand all mysteries and all knowledge, and though I have all faith, so that I could remove mountains, but have not love, I am nothing. And though I bestow all my goods to feed the poor, and though I give my body to be burned, but have not love, it profits me nothing – 1 Corinthians 13:1-3.

Finding God's heart and exploring its depths will bring us the greatest and sweetest satisfaction to be found on Earth. God is hated by many, so we won't always be popular. But the beat of His heart will put timely wisdom on our lips, intercession in our hearts, healing in our hands, and beautiful life-changing love in our every action.

Dear Lord, we thank You for leading us to Your amazing and mighty heart. Because it beats with forgiveness, mercy and grace, now our own will do the same.

Holiness

What Do You Think About?

...whatever things are true, whatever things are noble, whatever things are just, whatever things are pure, whatever things are lovely, whatever things are of good report, if there is any virtue and if there is anything praiseworthy: meditate on these things - Philippians 4:8.

Virtuous thoughts will clear a smooth, straight path between ourselves and the presence of God. Any human purity will be drawn like a magnet to the greater purity of our Lord, so this path will be well traveled. In contrast, negative and unclean thoughts are like rocks that cause us to stumble, fall, and be injured. These hazards either slow us down or prevent us from getting to God altogether.

Obviously, keeping our minds focused on positive, wholesome things will take serious commitment. Thankfully, the Spirit of God abiding in us is Holy, and He is our devoted Helper. He will correct us, guide us, and cheer us onward in our pursuit.

The rewards of thinking purely are many, but the greatest prize will be a closer connection to God. This nearness to Him brings increased energy, peace, and joy. People will notice a difference in us, and the Lord will be glorified.

I have rejoiced in the way of Your testimonies, as much as in all riches. I will meditate on Your precepts and contemplate Your ways. I will delight myself in Your statutes; I will not forget Your word - Psalm 119:14-16.

Yes, Lord, we will meditate on Your truth. We will contemplate the wonders of who You are as we move throughout each day. Thank You for inspiring us from within by Your Spirit and from without by Your beautiful creation.

Reaping What We Sow

November 22, 2006

Do not be deceived, God is not mocked; for whatever a man sows, that he will also reap. For he who sows to his flesh will of the flesh reap corruption, but he who sows to the Spirit will of the Spirit reap everlasting life. And let us not grow weary while doing good, for in due season we shall reap if we do not lose heart - Galatians 6:7-9.

<u>Do not be deceived</u>.   These four words are critical. Too many Christians have gradually stepped into subtle sins that have not-so-subtle consequences. Don't ever forget that Satan convinced brilliant, holy angels to rebel against God, with catastrophic results. He is up to the same tricks here on Earth—and now within the church.

<u>For he who sows to his flesh will of the flesh reap corruption</u>. Trying to satisfy our physical and emotional needs outside of God's parameters certainly qualifies us to reap the spoils of corruption. Overindulgence or addiction of any kind leads to destruction. Putting material gain ahead of spiritual prosperity will leave us impoverished. Deciding we can do anything without the blessing and help of God is downright foolish.

<u>But he who sows to the Spirit will of the Spirit reap everlasting life</u>.   We can wisely choose this path every morning. Pursuing the love, truth, and power of God through His Word and His Spirit is vital to doing His will. Every honorable choice and every righteous sacrifice is a powerful seed that we sow. And the harvest we reap is finer than any treasure the world has to offer.

<u>And let us not grow weary while doing good</u>.   Maybe you've been waiting a long time to reap some important harvests. Spiritual battles can get intense, and you would really enjoy some rest. Or perhaps you've experienced a difficult loss and don't know the reason why. What better time than right now to listen for the voice of God who whispers to us all? *Come closer. Come into My presence. I AM who you need. Now is the season to reap from My heart.*

Thank you, Lord, for Your warnings of deception. Teach us to always sow wisely and at the proper times. We call on Your mercy each day.

Choose Life

July 27, 2006

I call heaven and earth as witnesses today against you, that I have set before you life and death, blessing and cursing; therefore choose life, that both you and your descendants may live... - Deuteronomy 30:19.

I recently taped a sign to the center of my television screen. In large letters it says "choose life." TV programming isn't what it used to be; therefore, much of it should be avoided by Christians who pursue holiness. And yet I've struggled because television can be highly entertaining. It's especially appealing when I'm lonely or tired. So, the sign on my TV is a reminder that watching vulgar sitcoms and brutal dramas that cheapen the value of life is the same as choosing death.

- Our days are filled with choices. We can give and receive blessings, or we can give and receive curses.

- Every choice will affect the ones we love. Whether good or evil, the things we select will eventually touch every person in our realm of influence.

The message of Deuteronomy 30:19 is simple, yet powerful. Please take a moment to read it again and let the meaning sink in. Let me challenge you to memorize this verse, then make some "choose life" signs. God will tell you where to put them.

Thank You, Lord, for not forcing Your will upon us. You show great respect by allowing us to choose for ourselves. We all need Your grace to choose wisely. Please let us see with Your perspective.

Passing Through Valleys

Hard times come as a result of sin and poor choices, but they will also come from the Lord as a form of testing. No matter the cause, He will always be glorified in these situations if we respond properly to the adversity.

Will we turn to the world or to God for help? Will we praise Him, or will we murmur and complain? Will we obey, even when this prolongs our discomfort? Will we turn to God immediately or only after we've tried it "our way"? Are we willing to learn patience, humility, and the holy art of "waiting on the Lord"?

Whatever the source of our difficulties, the response should be the same—to glorify God by turning to Him for guidance, protection, and provision.

As they pass through the Valley of Baca, they make it a spring; The rain also covers it with pools – Psalm 84:6.

The word, baca, means "weeping." As we pass through places that are severe enough to make us cry, we must remember the Holy One who wants to comfort and refresh us. When we draw near to the Lord and abide in His presence, our "valley" becomes a place of beauty for ourselves and for others. I was recently pondering this verse when the Spirit explained that the Lord *is* the spring. As I draw near to Him for refreshing each day, I can expect to move deeper into His presence. I can be immersed in God the same as I would be immersed in a pool of deep, pure water.

While I was thinking of the valleys I've walked through during my life, the Spirit spoke to me clearly. He told me that my years of difficulty have not been wasted time because He has brought a level of holiness into my life. Then He spoke of the high value God assigns to holiness —it is a beautiful thing and is greatly prized by Him. He is always pleased when testing results in purity.

Pursue peace with all people, and holiness, without which no one will see the Lord... - Hebrews 12:14.

As it turns out, hard times are a gateway to the holiness God desires for us—and holiness leads to consistent time in His presence.

We thank You, Lord, for the stepping stones and pathways that lead us to You, even when they detour through valleys. Hardship would never be our choice, so You choose this for us when it's necessary for growth. We submit to Your plans because we trust You and know You good.

Holiness Brings Change

January 14, 2006

How strong is your passion to please the Lord through your holiness? Jesus had an intense desire to please the Father in this way. Because of perfect holiness, Jesus enjoyed a wonderful closeness with the Father and was given clear insight into His will. This discernment gave Him direction for prayer and miracles. Jesus displayed extraordinary power while living as a man, here on Earth. He set an exciting and realistic example for Christians to follow.

For us in the world today, choosing holiness requires great courage and humility. We must be in love with the Lord to even desire this trait, and only with the Holy Spirit are we able to walk such an elevated path.

A highway shall be there, and a road, and it shall be called the highway of Holiness. The unclean shall not pass over it, but it shall be for others. Whoever walks the road, although a fool, shall not go astray. No lion shall be there, nor shall any ravenous beast go up on it; it shall not be found there. But the redeemed shall walk there... - Isaiah 35:8-9.

Holiness is not being squeaky-clean and legalistically following the rules. Holiness happens when we spend time with God. It awakens us to the life of Christ within, so we receive revelation knowledge instead of merely compiling facts. Holiness is admitting our weakness and submitting to the powerful grace of God. Holiness is a key that opens doors to change.

Holiness will continue unveiling itself, far into eternity.

Give to the LORD the glory due His name; bring an offering, and come before Him. Oh, worship the LORD in the beauty of holiness! - 1 Chronicles 16:29.

Dear Lord, please increase our desire to be holy, just as You are holy. Stir up our hearts to give You pleasure through our purity. Make us increasingly aware of Your abiding Presence, and make us sensitive to Your will.

Face to Face

February 4, 2008

Meeting God face to face would be a life-changing encounter. Our hearts and minds would never be the same. Seeing who God really is would make us acutely aware of our own condition, just like the prophet, Isaiah, who quickly repented of his sin and was cleansed by a coal from the altar:

So I said: "Woe is me, for I am undone! Because I am a man of unclean lips, and I dwell in the midst of a people of unclean lips; for my eyes have seen the King, the LORD of hosts." Then one of the seraphim flew to me, having in his hand a live coal which he had taken with the tongs from the altar. And he touched my mouth with it, and said: "Behold, this has touched your lips; your iniquity is taken away, and your sin purged" - Isaiah 6:5-7.

As we learn from Isaiah, seeing "the King" is a deeply humbling, almost crushing experience. But we must not be deterred from drawing near. Just as with Isaiah, God wants to meet with us, and He will not crush the ones He died for.

As we draw near to God, He will draw near to us (James 4:8). We don't need to be perfect to approach Him, but a strong desire for holiness is required. We're told to cleanse our hands and purify our hearts. The cleansing and purification are essentially acts of drawing near.

There is much beauty and glory to be seen of God within our spirit that doesn't include seeing His actual face and form. But I am convinced that here on Earth, if we desire it enough, our eyes will see the King, just as Isaiah did. This may happen in the spirit realm, but that is just as real as the physical, if not more so.

God blesses those whose hearts are pure, for they will see God - Matthew 5:8 NLT.

We thank You, Lord, for seeking close connection with us. Thinking of Your desire for us is exciting—because You are exciting. Many of us have been blessed with a glimpse of Your glorious presence, but today we ask for more.

A Position of Power

What's the big deal about holiness? Do we really need to be good since Jesus already paid for our sin?

If you're truly born again, the Holy Spirit will lead you into ever-increasing purity. At some point, your grasp of holiness will reach beyond the simple concept of "good behavior." One day you'll experience the freedom and lightness that comes from close alignment with God. Great joy will come from pleasing Him.

If you strive to walk in holiness, then the kingdom of God—His mighty spiritual government and His righteous agenda—begins to take root in your thinking. You start to want what God wants. You begin to see with spiritual eyes and love with a circumcised heart (Deuteronomy 30:6). Irreversible changes occur within. There's no turning back.

Holiness helps you to fall more in love with God. You become His committed personal friend (Matthew 5:8), and He is pleased with your new-found motives. Your prayers are now pleasing to His ears. As holiness grows, it brings you to a position of power—to a place where God will move at your request. This is not because you've "earned" His attention, but because God has transformed you and carefully groomed you to work in agreement with Him.

And when the servant of the man of God arose early and went out, there was an army, surrounding the city with horses and chariots. And his servant said to him, "Alas, my master! What shall we do?" So he answered, "Do not fear, for those who are with us are more than those who are with them." And Elisha prayed, and said, "LORD, I pray, open his eyes that he may see." Then the LORD opened the eyes of the young man, and he saw. And behold, the mountain was full of horses and chariots of fire all around Elisha. So when the Syrians came down to him, Elisha prayed to the LORD, and said, "Strike this people, I pray, with blindness." And He struck them with blindness according to the word of Elisha – 2 Kings 6:15-18.

When Elisha prayed, God did as he asked. THAT is the big deal about holiness.

Most holy God, we thank You for placing within us the desire for purity. Thank You for making this possible through Your Word and by the precious blood of Jesus.

TRUTH

We Have the Light of Life

November 25, 2009

I find myself angered by the sin in this world, and you should too. It hurts us, and it hurts the ones we love. It robs us of blessings and causes much sorrow and pain. Even in its mildest forms, sin is an ugly perversion of the goodness of God. As a new Christian, I felt frustration and fear when facing the strongholds of evil around me. But now I know better. By His body and blood, the Lord has made us overcomers of this world. We grow in wisdom and power by His life within us. Abiding in Him, we can always be triumphant!

But you belong to God, my dear children. You have already won a victory over those people, because the Spirit who lives in you is greater than the spirit who lives in the world – 1 John 4:4 NLT.

God wants us living in His dominion of truth where we're no longer influenced by demonic lies—where we see problems as opportunities to tear down Satanic domains. We can live in the beautiful light of God. With Jesus, we have the Light of Life.

Then Jesus spoke to them again, saying, "I am the light of the world. He who follows Me shall not walk in darkness, but have the light of life" – John 8:12.

Thank You, Lord, for letting us live in Your light—displaying Your love, truth, and power throughout this world. Please open our eyes to the opportunities for ministry You set before us every day.

____

____

____

____

____

____

All Things Are New

July 2, 2007

Emotions are valuable gifts from God, both positive and negative. But Satan will exploit them if we're not on guard. One of the cruelest tricks of the enemy is to make us feel like something is wrong when everything is fine. Maybe we're stepping into a new level of faith, and we're pleasing the Lord by trusting Him. At this critical time the enemy tries to sabotage our efforts by dredging up old fears or memories of personal failure. The plan is to cause our behavior to align with those outdated feelings.

Or, we may be overly excited about something flashy and new, while ignoring a word from the Spirit to complete an unfinished project. This happens less often, but it's important to watch out for.

If we accept every thought or emotion as being valid, then we're in for quite a rough ride.

He who trusts in his own heart is a fool, but whoever walks wisely will be delivered – Proverbs 28:26.

Recently, while vacationing by myself, the enemy assaulted me with thoughts of "Oh, poor single me." Recognizing that I was under attack, I responded to every strike with a relevant truth, and I resisted the negative feelings. I had chosen to spend the week with God, so I was certainly not alone. The Holy Spirit gave me one uplifting word after another to extinguish the fiery darts. Because God's truth always prevails over evil, I was strengthened instead of wounded.

On the long drive home, the Holy Spirit had more encouragement for me. He supported my belief that abiding in Him keeps our failure in the past—never in the present or future. He applauded me for fighting properly during the week, and He blessed me with awareness of His love.

Therefore, if anyone is in Christ, he is a new creation; old things have passed away; behold, all things have become new – 2 Corinthians 5:17.

We have a new identity! We are new creatures with a glorious destiny
and future.

*What a wonderful God You are! A Father, Savior, and Comforting Spirit,
all together as One. We are never alone, and we can choose to be
victorious by Your grace.*

Christ in You

March 18, 2006

I pray that your hearts will be flooded with light so that you can understand the confident hope He has given to those He called— His holy people who are His rich and glorious inheritance. I also pray that you will understand the incredible greatness of God's power for us who believe Him. This is the same mighty power that raised Christ from the dead and seated him in the place of honor at God's right hand in the heavenly realms – Ephesians 1:18-20 NLT.

Within all of us is a realm of understanding. Inside this realm are many segments of truth, just like pieces of a jigsaw puzzle. When God knows we are ready, He connects a few of our puzzle pieces to display a larger, stronger portion of His truth. The beauty we see is familiar, but also fresh, new, and greater than before.

Sometimes the enemy blinds us to what is right beneath our nose, but God always restores the vision of those who want to see. He did this for me by connecting another piece of truth at a home-group meeting last night. My eyes were opened to a mission field that is very close at hand. Today I know that "Christ in me" has purposed to touch some needy people who are within my reach. My helping hands and my words of truth will be set on fire by God.

I'm well acquainted with the life-changing power of Christ within me, and after many personal victories, God has begun to change the nature of my battles. As He fits together more pieces of truth for me, His plans have become more challenging.

I urge you to submit to God and always be available. Let Him work His glorious wonders through you!

- Be diligent in seeking God and His truth.

- Humble yourself before Him, so He will enlarge your understanding.

- Know that His truth carries power for those who believe.

Thank You, Lord, for giving us truth as we need it. Thank You so much for working within us to apply it. You honor us with Your wisdom and understanding. Please keep our eyes bright, our ears sharp, and our spirits tuned to Your channel of truth and glory.

February 5, 2010

Walk in wisdom toward those who are outside, redeeming the time. Let your speech always be with grace, seasoned with salt, that you may know how you ought to answer each one - Colossians 4:5-6.

People caught in the snares of sin can be set completely free by hearing the truth about their predicament. Because Christians are the salt of the earth (Matthew 5:13), we're accountable for speaking truth when it's needed.

Salt has amazing properties. It seasons food, making flavors come alive. It also prevents our dehydration. It's vital for normal functioning of the human body. Salt can even save lives by killing germs. But we need to remember that salt will cause pain if sprinkled on an open wound. Those who are most in need of salt (truth) are the ones who may scream the loudest when it's applied.

Speaking truth to someone *must* be done in love. The Spirit may provide the perfect words right on the spot, but often we need to pray before we speak. I've been in situations where I had to pray for weeks before I was allowed to say a word.

Unless the need is urgent, I think salt is best applied in small doses over a period of time, making it acceptable to the recipient. A sprinkle here and a sprinkle there helps the hearer save face and avoid the sting of humiliation. It also gives them time to test-drive each new truth before they receive another.

Regrettably, no matter how careful and loving we may be, there will sometimes be strong reactions to the truth we speak. Anger, outrage, icy silence, and even retaliation are normal responses from the prisoners of sin. But if we've followed the Lord's direction, we needn't worry. The Word and the Spirit will have their intended effect.

When we ourselves are wounded by the sinner's reaction, we must cling to God and His love for us. We don't need to lose sight of the task at hand. Just like Jesus, we will experience times of rejection because of speaking truth. So, we need to remember—*it's not about us.* It's about setting the captives free.

Truth, beautiful truth! Jesus, I'm speaking of You—the Way, the Truth, and the Life (John 14:6). Your truth surely guides, teaches, imparts, and enables us. We are only "salt" because we have You!

The Beautiful Mind of Christ

July 18, 2018

For "who has known the mind of the LORD that he may instruct Him?" But we have the mind of Christ – 1 Corinthians 2:16.

Every born-again Christian has been given the beautiful mind of Christ. When His Spirit comes to live in our hearts, He also inhabits our minds. I dearly love the fact that Jesus "thinks in me."

In the beginning was the Word, and the Word was with God, and the Word was God – John 1:1.

Because the Word was and is God, then it stands to reason that the mind of Christ, who *is* God, is filled with scripture—often reminding us of truth to fit our current need. When we have read and understood a particular scripture, God may retrieve it from our subconscious memory, even years later, and lovingly hand it to us as a gift in our time of need. He may even put a specific "spin" on its application that we would not have perceived on our own.

The entrance of Your words gives light; it gives understanding to the simple – Psalm 119:130.

Each one of us is simple-minded without the presence of God. Apart from Him, our intellect is like a scrap of paper tossed in the wind. But joined with God, we have mental and spiritual genius. We soon understand that all negative thoughts are noisy, discordant intruders. We find that ignoring them sharpens our focus on the power and goodness of our Creator. We begin hearing the symphonies of His Word and the melodies of His heart. Here are a few examples:

<u>Revelation</u>: The mind of Christ imparts revelation, and this leads to greater understanding. His thoughts come to us like refreshing drops of rain on a hot afternoon. Being quite different than our own human reasoning, the mentality of God carries vibrant life. All of a sudden, we "know." We're enlightened and helped by God's powerful disclosure. The more we expect this, the more we will experience it.

Inspiration: The brilliant thoughts of our mighty God provide inspiration. We're given words of encouragement for ourselves and others, as well as bright ideas to put into action. The mind and heart of the Lord stir up His fire within us. *Creativity is unleashed!* We're better able to show His love to the hurting world around us.

Protection: As a mighty "secret weapon," the indwelling thoughts of God work to protect us. A few days ago, just before bedtime, the Lord prompted me to check the cruise control on my car. This after-market accessory drains the battery if it's switched on too long while the car isn't being driven. Sure enough, the cruise control was on, so I turned it off and thanked God for the timely reminder. This kept me from missing a morning appointment. Our Lord cares about the little things. It's always good to listen because the issue at hand may turn out to be quite large. We may have swallowed a poisonous lie, and God is offering His antidote of truth.

Knowing God: Over time, connection to the mind of our Lord is how we get to know Him. His wise and loving thoughts are a window into His heart. We can choose to heed His voice—to drink deeply from the well of His beauty and love. This helps us to love Him in return by receiving, obeying, thanking, and praising Him. He gave us His *all*, so let us do the same.

Think over what I say, for the Lord will give you understanding in everything – 2 Timothy 2:7 ESV.

Thank You, Lord, for the priceless gift of Your mind. Thank You for the endless depth of treasure that You are. Let us never forget Your gift or take Your presence for granted. Help us to stay in this secret place of intimacy throughout our days—never turning aside.

No Fear

The Season to Decree

September 25, 2018

"Today is a good day for decrees!" That is exactly what the Lord said when I first woke on a recent morning.

He spoke this to me primarily regarding physical ailments. As we grow older, they seem to increase in number and severity. The world says these disorders are natural and should be expected. But God once said clearly to me, *"You don't have to accept these things."* His voice of direction to me is profusely backed up in the Word.

But He was wounded for our transgressions, He was bruised for our iniquities; The chastisement for our peace was upon Him, and by His stripes we are healed – Isaiah 53:5.

Because the world despises us, our Father wants to make a grand display of His love for us through healing:

"For I will restore health to you, and I will heal your wounds," says the LORD, "because they have called you an outcast, saying, 'This is Zion, whom no one seeks after and for whom no one cares!' " – Jeremiah 30:17.

We're responsible to pray for and decree God's will concerning our families and the rest of our assigned domain. As always, Earth is our training ground for what lies ahead in eternity.

Let's bless the Lord by expecting and receiving His healing for us. Through faith, let's open wide the gates for His truth and glory to flow. Yes! Today is a good day for us to decree! We can start with declarations of health, then move on to statements regarding our relationships, finances, and the harvest of souls.

Thank You, Lord, for Your tremendous, bountiful love! Thank You for speaking clearly to all who will listen. We want to move forward in Your kingdom and have our lives to be a blessing to You. Please give us Your favor, Lord, so we can show favor to others.

I Am Healed

July 31, 2017

Beloved, I pray that you may prosper in all things and be in health, just as your soul prospers - 3 John 2.

Over the years I've fallen hard a few times, always landing on my left hip. This caused damage that led to severe deterioration of the joint. On September 9, 2009, I had total hip replacement surgery on my left side. I prayed a lot before the surgery, and the Lord gave me a vision concerning the outcome. He showed me a picture of surgical tools cutting into human flesh, then He showed me a swimming pool with underwater lights on. I felt sure of the meaning of this vision. The surgical tools and flesh represented the surgery, and the swimming pool was symbolic of the pool of Bethesda (John 5) where healing took place. The light in the pool symbolized God's presence and power. I believed God was telling me to go ahead with the surgery, and that He would bring complete healing.

The Holy Spirit often tells us things ahead of time so we'll have His assurance to carry us through a trial. This was definitely the case with my hip surgery because the surgeon made a serious error. When I first tried to stand, I knew that something wasn't right. My legs were no longer equal in length. My left leg was about three quarters of an inch longer than my right leg. The doctor had corrected one problem but also created another.

If I wanted to live with anger, there was plenty to fuel this fire. The surgeon's attitude about the outcome was absolutely flippant and unsympathetic. My overall recovery was hindered by the mismatched length of my legs, so I had half-inch wedges built into the soles of all shoes for my right foot, and I supplemented that with quarter-inch inserts, bringing the total amount of lift to three-quarters of an inch. Though I refused to sulk and be angry, I was *not* happy with the situation. As a woman of faith I refused to accept it.

I remembered the vision the Lord had given me, and that is what I fervently pursued. I read "Smith Wigglesworth on Healing," a book that is full of healing testimony and scripture that supports healing miracles. Every time I was tempted to be upset, I thanked God for my healing. I thanked Him for my legs being equal in length. I said out loud, "By Jesus' stripes I am (already) healed!" On some days, I said this often.

But He was wounded for our transgressions, He was bruised for our iniquities; the chastisement for our peace was upon Him, and by His stripes <u>we are healed</u> – Isaiah 53:5.

A few weeks after my surgery I had some mature Christian friends lay hands on me and pray for my healing to manifest. I was disappointed at not seeing or feeling a difference, but I chose to continue believing for complete healing. I *knew* God wanted my legs to be the same length.

One day in late July, 2017—eight years after the surgery—I heard of a seminar at "River at Tampa Bay" in Florida. This was Rodney Howard-Browne's church. I vaguely remembered that he was a healer, so I did some online research. Within hours, the Spirit had stirred me to drive the seven hours and attend a couple meetings. Dr. Brown didn't minister to me during the first meeting, and I was dismayed. Though I was also determined. Before the next meeting, I asked to see an associate pastor. This man took me into an office and prayed over me. I watched as my legs become perfectly even. A few days after I returning home, I found that my painful knees were also healed.

Today my legs are exactly the same length, thanks to Jesus' suffering on my behalf. My faith combined with the faith of other Christians has brought a miracle of healing to my body. My interpretation of the vision God gave me was accurate.

Most assuredly, I say to you, he who believes in Me, the works that I do he will do also; and greater works than these he will do, because I go to My Father. And whatever you ask in My name, that I will do, that the Father may be glorified in the Son. If you ask anything in My name, I will do it - John 14:12-14.

Thank You, Lord, for healing Your children. We are grateful for Your touch! You have created us beautifully, and You desire to keep us well. And once again, dear Lord, I say, "Thank You for healing ME."

April 4, 2008

I awoke one morning with a flurry of concern swirling in my mind. Looming ahead were issues I soon would have to deal with. I began to meditate on what God had already told me about the coming year, and it wasn't long before He spoke: *"They're only giants."*

Now, that almost sounds like sarcasm, but I knew it wasn't. The message was music to my ears. With three words, God let me know I have nothing to fear. The changes ahead may look too hard to handle, but they're only "giants of the land" (Joshua 12:4), and they can be easily slain by faith. Just as God told Joshua before he crossed the Jordan to claim the promised land, He tells us all today:

Be strong and of good courage; do not be afraid, nor be dismayed, for the LORD your God is with you wherever you go - Joshua 1:9.

The giants we face are not always people. Sometimes they're new circumstances that are strange and as yet "unconquered." The story of Joshua reveals the heart of God toward every Christian. If He tells us to go somewhere, we can rest assured that He goes with us. We will surely encounter giants along the way, and we can always view them as something to sharpen our teeth on. With God by our side, how could they possibly hurt us?

For you will cross over the Jordan and go in to possess the land which the LORD your God is giving you, and you will possess it and dwell in it - Deuteronomy 11:31.

Amen! I like the sound of that!

Thank You, dear Lord, for making it clear to us where we stand. When You say, "They're only giants," this tells us how big and powerful we are when facing the enemy. With You by our side, those demons are squashed like bugs beneath our feet. We have nothing to be afraid of!

If We Faint Not

July 8, 2006

Evil spirits are the ultimate con artists. These fraudulent beings depend on trickery, betrayal, and every sort of lie to disarm our potential and turn us away from God. A common but very effective lie is that "nothing will ever change"—that we will have to live with our present pain, hardship, or trouble until the day we die. This lie alleges that God does not care and cannot be trusted. Once it is firmly established, the deception is a cancer that cruelly kills.

To combat the lies, we must read the Word and constantly hear how much God cares (Romans 10:17). We need to read each one of His wonderful feats on our behalf—of the lengths He goes for us. And we need to learn His plans for our future.

A season of warfare is upon us, and we are called to fight. The Sword of the Spirit—the Word of God—is an unbeatable weapon.

Apathy is not an option. Remember what God says about being "lukewarm" (Revelation 3:16). We must be on guard and always ready for battle—never yielding to self-pity or fear. Let's resolve to study the Word, learn what is true, and turn to God in prayer with all attacks of negative thought. He will protect what is ours and bless us even further. We'll have peace in the midst of battles and victories at every turn. Our minds and spirits will be strong and never near to giving up.

If we faint not, then we'll reap the fruit of our hope! We will gain all that God has promised because He never ceases to be faithful (Galatians 6:9).

The thief does not come except to steal, and to kill, and to destroy. I have come that they may have life, and that they may have it more abundantly - John 10:10.

Thank You, Lord, that we don't have to be afraid. As we rest in You, life always changes for the better. We're never stuck in a place of hopelessness and fear. If we listen, we'll always hear Your "songs of deliverance" (Psalm 32:7). Lord, You are so good for giving us promises of hope. With You, there is no fear!

God Is With Us!

I'm praising God all day today and maybe for all of the week! He deftly won a battle for me this morning. I was completely helpless, and if not for the Lord's intervention, the results could have been quite negative. Instead, I was favored and given respect.

I've known for days that a conflict was coming, and I watched as the storm approached. Clouds of manipulation and strife rolled in—things that God really hates, and things I've grown to detest. When the tempest hit, I was surprised by its ferocity. But my preparation in prayer brought a swift and decisive triumph. This attacking force was no match for the power of God. Yes, a mountain was moved for me today, and I want to shout about it!

What can you gain from my short testimony that is lacking in any detail? Start by accepting my excitement over God's miraculous intervention. (And understand that details are not appropriate.) Then, apply the basics of my testimony to any future situation of your own. If you know that an enemy has set an unfair trap for you—one that will work quite well if God doesn't get involved—then ask God to get involved!

Take counsel together, but it will come to nothing; speak the word, but it will not stand, for God is with us. For the LORD spoke thus to me with a strong hand, and instructed me that I should not walk in the way of this people, saying: "Do not say, 'A conspiracy,' concerning all that this people call a conspiracy, nor be afraid of their threats, nor be troubled. The LORD of hosts, Him you shall hallow; let Him be your fear, and let Him be your dread. He will be as a sanctuary, but a stone of stumbling and a rock of offense to both the houses of Israel, as a trap and a snare to the inhabitants of Jerusalem – Isaiah 8:10-14.

Dear sweet Lord, we thank You for the beauty of Your involvement in our lives. In defense of our righteous behavior, You tell the enemy, "Do your best—then die!" You are completely awesome!

Focus on the Good

June 29, 2009

If four things didn't happen the way we wanted, and one thing has blessed us, then we must keep our focus on the blessing. The fact is, God is in control. The enemy loves to exaggerate the size of our problems, hoping we won't see them as "opportunities," and hoping we won't notice the grace involved in the thing that blessed us. So instead of falling into an emotional trap, we need to ask ourselves, "What does God say about this? What has He promised in His word? What good news has the Spirit been whispering?"

We need not waste our energy fretting about tomorrow or defending ourselves against selfish people. God sees and hears all things. He knows exactly what's going on, and He's our strong defense in times of trouble. We know He works all things together for our good (Romans 8:28). Because of this, we're free to focus on kingdom assignments. We should be moving ahead at a steady pace instead of getting mired in strife and fear. We must always focus on God and think of His goodness.

Be anxious for nothing, but in everything by prayer and supplication, with thanksgiving, let your requests be made known to God; and the peace of God, which surpasses all understanding, will guard your hearts and minds through Christ Jesus. Finally, brethren, whatever things are true, whatever things are noble, whatever things are just, whatever things are pure, whatever things are lovely, whatever things are of good report, if there is any virtue and if there is anything praiseworthy—meditate on these things - Philippians 4:6-8.

Dear God, You are so good! Everything from You is either blessing or opportunity. Let Your Spirit remind us of that each day. Let us see this world as the "training for eternity" that it is.

All is Well

April 30, 2009

Do you ever feel weak and alone and afraid? It's important to turn to God when this happens and hear what He has to say. When I talk to the Lord about my own weaknesses and fears, He tells me it doesn't matter because He is strong on my behalf. As long as I trust Him, I'll be safe and secure. He assures me that "all is well."

Because I'm single, I sometimes feel alone. I don't have family nearby who accept me just as I am, warts and all. But the Holy Spirit reminds me that God is my family. He tells me quite often that I am His beloved.

...we know how dearly God loves us, because He has given us the Holy Spirit to fill our hearts with His love - Romans 5:5.

As we all know, fear can be persistent. Sometimes it will follow in my footsteps, nagging me from close behind. Or it will jump ahead to frighten me face to face. But God has shown me clearly that fear is only a "paper tiger." This emotion, however valid it may seem, is based on flimsy lies. It cannot hurt me unless I overreact, which of course is the enemy's goal.

Do not fear, little flock, for it is your Father's good pleasure to give you the kingdom - Luke 12:32.

Yes, the kingdom of God is ours. The battles are already won, and every giant has already been defeated. We may be weak, but we're never alone. The strength of God is always by our side.

Fear not, for I am with you; Be not dismayed, for I am your God. I will strengthen you, Yes, I will help you, I will uphold you with My righteous right hand – Isaiah 41:10.

Thank You, Lord, that I am never without You. I love to watch Your glorious strength from my place of weakness. You're exactly what I need! Oh, what a wonderful God I have!

Embrace God's Peace

September 5, 2010

Now is the time to live by faith—to cast off fear and embrace God's peace. It's time to make up your mind. Will you resist every tormenting thought from the enemy? Will you seek God and His Word to thereby live in His victory? From this day forward, let this be so. It's time to focus on God's truth instead of on what you imagine or feel.

For the weapons of our warfare are not carnal but mighty in God for pulling down strongholds, casting down arguments and every high thing that exalts itself against the knowledge of God, bringing every thought into captivity to the obedience of Christ... - 2 Corinthians 10:4-5.

God recently showed me a picture of demonic hands reaching through iron bars. From behind those restraining bars, demons were trying to grab Christians and draw them into a place of distress—a place where their minds would dwell on negativity and be consumed with depression and fear. The message in this scene is that demonic hands can only "grab us" if we walk within their reach. We must not consort with evil.

Saints, we should be walking closely with God, listening to His wise and beautiful voice. This is a choice we can always make.

Blessed is the man who trusts in the LORD and whose hope is the LORD. For he shall be like a tree planted by the waters, which spreads out its roots by the river, and will not fear when heat comes; but its leaf will be green, and will not be anxious in the year of drought, nor will cease from yielding fruit – Jer. 17:7-8.

We are certainly blessed if we trust in the Lord and make Him the focus of our hope. Will you do this today? Will you put down roots in rich soil and produce good fruit for the Kingdom?

Thank You, Lord, that we need not succumb to fear. Thank You for Your living Word. It lights our way to safety and peace—a glorious place that resonates with Your love. Thank You for teaching us Your holy ways so we can feel at home with You.

Who Do We Trust?

February 5, 2012

**But we had the sentence of death in ourselves, that we should not trust in ourselves, but in God which raiseth the dead –
2 Corinthians 1:9.**

Are you at the end of your rope? Are you caught between a rock and a hard place? These phrases describe in modern terms what the apostle Paul refers to as "the sentence of death in ourselves." No matter what we call it, being at the complete mercy of God can be an uncomfortable place if our faith isn't razor sharp.

Some of us may think our faith is strong. But when we're put in a place where God is our only hope, we quickly find our faith confronted by various forms of fear. *Have I heard the Lord correctly? Has He changed His mind? Why is this happening to me? Did I mess things up last week?* Anxiety may rise with us each morning, forcing us to engage in spiritual battle before we're out of bed. But if fear pushes us closer to the Lord, then we must thank Him for allowing every frightful thought.

The presence of anxiety exposes our sin of independence from God, and we must repent of this. Yes, it's true that fear comes from Satan, but God will use it to show us our desperate need for Him. (I'm sure God enjoys using Satan's fear campaign against him.)

In His mercy, God doesn't too often give us a "sentence of death in ourselves." And when He does, He's waiting to "raise us from death" (deliver us from evil) and make a display of His glory.

Voicing our thanks and praise to God will unleash His power and purpose. Offering praise in the midst of testing may be difficult, but we can do it. Just remember the examples set by Joseph, David, and Paul. These men were victorious because of their trust in God. And as we're tested by Him today, we can do the same. Like the saints before us, our courageous lives will bless the world. But most importantly, we'll bless the heart of God.

Father, please teach us to trust You completely. Whatever that takes, we submit to Your methods. Yes, we submit to Your love.

I Sought the Lord

June 7, 2016

The Spirit, the Word, and personal experience have taught me that God is always good and always faithful. I've received many bright and unique promises for this life on Earth. My cup will never be half empty. It will always overflow. I won't be preaching "end-times gloom and doom" to those in my sphere of influence.

I know that God is present with me, and I expect His power and His blessings to accompany Him. I look for signs and wonders—for a broad array of miracles. The misguided can anticipate darkness and poverty, but I will look for the loving face of God and His generous, outstretched hands.

I will praise the LORD at all times. I will constantly speak his praises. I will boast only in the LORD; let all who are helpless take heart. Come, let us tell of the LORD's greatness; let us exalt his name together – Psalm 34:1-3 NLT.

Of course darkness is real, and it can be disconcerting, but it doesn't stop the presence and power of God (Job 42:2). The Word is still alive and active—still sharper than a two-edged sword (Hebrews 4:12). The Word from God's mouth will never return to Him in defeat, but will always accomplish His pleasure and His purpose (Isaiah 55:11). Always! God is still sovereign. He is still the Most High over all the Earth (Psalm 97:9).

When darkness comes, we can worship God like a psalmist (Psalm 100). We can be brave like Joshua (Joshua 1:9). We can do anything but dwell upon the dark.

I sought the LORD, and He heard me, and delivered me from all my fears. They looked to Him and were radiant, and their faces were not ashamed. This poor man cried out, and the LORD heard him, and saved him out of all his troubles. The angel of the LORD encamps all around those who fear Him, and delivers them – Psalm 34:4-7.

Dear Lord, please fill us with a passion to know Your heart!

Fear No Evil

August 21, 2010

Yea, though I walk through the valley of the shadow of death, I will fear no evil; For You are with me; Your rod and Your staff, they comfort me - Psalm 23:4.

Many Christians think of "the valley of the shadow of death" as that final time on Earth when we lay on our death bead. Others think of it as a dangerous situation where physical death is a real possibility. We've probably heard these definitions in a sermon or read them in a book. They're certainly not incorrect. But the Holy Spirit recently showed me a broader view:

Life is from God, but death and destruction are from Satan. Therefore, the "shadow of death" is the shadow of Satan's influence, however great or small. For example, someone living in a home with an alcoholic is living in the shadow of death. Or a woman employed in an oppressive environment is working in the shadow of death. If we're not in close contact with the Lord or protected by Him through prayer, this shadow can be destructive.

God can use the shadows to draw us closer into His loving arms. In the safety of His embrace, He prepares us for what lies ahead. Quite often, the Lord takes us into the valleys for the sole purpose of "cleaning house" and routing the enemy.

While in this valley, getting the lay of the land, we may try to adjust to the problems and tolerate the sin. But the presence of Christ in us will never be at peace with any amount of darkness. The time will come to boldly pull out our weapons of truth and light.

As we combat the evil of this world, it's important to remember: The shadows of death are not cast by human flesh but by the "rulers of darkness" (Ephesians 6:12). Difficult people must be handled with love, while the underlying demonic influence is met with our sharpest weapons. We dare not compromise. We are called to be skilled enforcers of God's will.

Have I not commanded you? Be strong and courageous. Do not be terrified; do not be discouraged, for the LORD your God will be with you wherever you go" - Joshua 1:9.

God repeats this message throughout His Word: We need not be afraid. He is always with us, no matter how large and dark the shadows.

Your presence, Lord, is the perfect protection from evil. Your tender care for those You love sends a chill down the enemy's spine. We thank You for every shadow that pushes us closer to You. And we thank You for Your beautiful light that makes the darkness flee.

May 30, 2011

For the weapons of our warfare are not carnal, but mighty through God to the pulling down of strong holds; casting down imaginations, and every high thing that exalteth itself against the knowledge of God, and bringing into captivity every thought to the obedience of Christ... - 2 Corinthians 10:4-5 KJV.

Let's look at "imaginations." The Amplified Classic Bible calls them "arguments and theories and reasonings." I think of them as "the fiery darts of the wicked one" (Ephesians 6:16). However we interpret the word, evil imaginations are sent to torment our minds and steal from our future. Imaginations come disguised as our own thoughts, seeming reasonable and probably true. They often present worst-case scenarios, so they set us up for worry, anxiety, and full-blown fear.

If the enemy can engulf us with anxiety about the future, then we're more likely to make a mess of things this afternoon. Therefore, to protect us, the Lord tells us to focus on today, and take no thought for tomorrow (Matthew 6:34).

Through God, we must cast down every imagination that has come to steal what He has given us. We must tap into the riches of God's mind (1 Corinthians 2:16). When abiding in the Lord and hearing His thoughts, we are strengthened (Nehemiah 8:10, Psalm 21:1, and Psalm 29:11).

Why do the nations rage, and the people plot a vain thing? ...He who sits in the heavens shall laugh; The Lord shall hold them in derision - Psalm 2:1-4.

When we're in tune with the mind of God, we can laugh along with Him when people around us "plot a vain thing." I've been asking the Lord to fill my mind with what He's thinking. There's no better way to feel good.

Be anxious for nothing, but in everything by prayer and supplication, with thanksgiving, let your requests be made known to God; and the peace of God, which surpasses all understanding, will guard your hearts and minds through Christ Jesus. Finally, brethren, whatever things are true, whatever

things are noble, whatever things are just, whatever things are pure, whatever things are lovely, whatever things are of good report, if there is any virtue and if there is anything praiseworthy—meditate on these things - Philippians 4:6-8.

Thank You, Lord, for Your continuous salvation. Every day we're saved from snares because of Your presence within. Thank You for Your beautiful mind. When we're obedient to Your words, they lead us safely along the path of sanctification.

Don't Be Afraid

April 27, 2006

God will tell us wonderful things, then test us on what we've heard. We'll find ourselves immersed in vivid realities that are both frightening and exciting. Weak and stumbling at first, we will eventually succeed through God's indwelling power.

For whatever is born of God overcomes the world. And this is the victory that has overcome the world—our faith - 1 John 5:4.

The enemy will be vicious. He works hard to build walls of distrust between us and God, bombarding us with lies meant to overwhelm us with fear. As scary as this may sound, God only allows the nasty behavior of Satan when it will ultimately work for our good. The evil one may be smarter than us, but he's *nothing* compared to our Lord. Abiding in Christ is our perfect protection, carrying us through every danger. We truly have nothing to fear.

Christian virtues like patience and humility aren't much fun to acquire because they're always severely tested. Yes, when people mistreat us, God requires that we respond gracefully. And we're met with many lies, flowing from the lips of those we learn to pray for. Being filled with the Spirit is the only way to move victoriously through this

...He was a murderer from the beginning, not holding to the truth, for there is no truth in him. When he lies, he speaks his native language, for he is a liar and the father of lies - John 8:44 NIV.

Yes, Satan is a liar—just a dirty puff of smoke. We needn't be tricked into overreacting or getting derailed from God's purpose. On the contrary, we can learn the truth, and let every lie remind us of God.

We praise You, Lord, for the truth You speak so fluently. Your words guide us through every storm and every dark night—through every testing of our faith. Your whispers encourage and comfort us as we step out of the boat and onto the water. Thank You so much for letting Your truth brighten our lives!

HIS TOUCH

Live Like It's True

I love the line in the 1991 movie, City Slickers, when Billy Crystal tells his downhearted friend, "Your life is a do-over. You've got a clean slate." Hmmm. That sounds like something from the heart of God. In fact, it is:

His mercies never come to an end; they are new every morning - Lamentations 3:22-23 ESV.

When we wake up each day, we get a "do-over." That's just how our Lord is. People may hold grudges, but the mercies of God are new every morning. His mercy toward us is so zealous and intense that He sent His Son to die in payment for our sin.

The blood of Jesus is powerful! It wipes our slate completely clean.

As far as the east is from the west, so far has He removed our transgressions from us - Psalm 103:12.

God's amazing grace is ours to claim, every minute of every day. His forgiveness, removal, and forgetting of our sin is proof that He's on our side. His love for us proclaims that we're very special in His eyes—that each new day is filled with promise and glory.

Even as we walk through hazardous, painful places—through knee-deep garbage with enemy lies whizzing past our heads—we are surrounded by God's favor.

For You, O LORD, will bless the righteous; with favor You will surround him as with a shield - Psalm 5:12.

Oh, yes! As beloved children of the Most High God, we live with incredible favor. Will you dare to believe this good news? Will you rise up in faith and live like it's true?

Your mercies are new every morning! Our sins are removed! You bless us and surround us with favor! Thank You, Lord!

March 7, 2016

When I get alone with God and praise Him out loud, the Spirit will often help by giving me words. During a recent time of early morning worship, the Spirit prompted me to thank the Lord for "directing the steps of my heart." I recorded the phrase in my journal because it seems significant. Now I'm becoming aware of how God leads my heart on a regular basis.

Christians are cautioned to not take action based on emotion, and that *sounds* like good advice. But the Spirit undeniably leads us with Godly desire and love. Certainly, we must not act on human impulse, but when God orchestrates our moves with the beat of His own heart, we would be foolish not to follow.

A few days ago, I found myself doing something that would have been too difficult if not for the tremendous pull of God's love for someone. In my heart where He abides, I simply had no choice.

Anyone who does not love does not know God, because God is love – 1 John 4:8 ESV.

As sheep, we know the voice of our Shepard. And as the bride of Christ, we know the heart of our Beloved. Let us always respond to His call.

Your voice, Lord, is unmistakable. Thank You for directing the steps of our hearts where otherwise we wouldn't dare to go.

Today Is the Day

November 12, 2015

How often do you think of times gone by, wishing you could go back and do a few things differently? Or do you look backwards with longing to circumstances that were a lot more comfortable? God has blessed us with a capacity to remember our past, but He doesn't want us dwelling there.

TODAY is a glorious gift from the Lord! Every minute of it!

This is the day the Lord has made; we will rejoice and be glad in it - Psalm 118:24.

Christians don't need to look backward with either longing or regret. And we certainly don't need to be stagnant, allowing yesterday to dictate what happens today. Every new day is filled with tremendous potential for growth and change.

Therefore, if anyone is in Christ, he is a new creation. The old has passed away; behold, the new has come – 2 Corinthians 5:17 ESV.

Did you hear that?

You are a new creation!
The old has passed away!
All things have become new!

I think it's time to do a happy dance! And while we dance, we can sing our praise to God for the wonderful day ahead. And as long as we're singing to the Lord, we should do it very loud so the enemy can hear it too.

Lord, please give us Your perspective. Let us say "good bye" to the past. We want to embrace today with all the blessing it holds. And let us look to the future with much anticipation.

____

____

Memories

December 7, 2015

A special "Hi" to all the baby-boomers reading this. We are privileged to have been born at a wonderful time in history. Ours has been a unique era in which simplicity crashed head-on with industry and technology.

I have vivid memories of my early years. Living on a 140-acre Indiana farm meant that Mama still churned butter, but she had the option of buying something new It was called "Oleo." Our family was fairly independent, and the farm was self-supporting—echoing the rural lifestyle of centuries past. But we did have a modern black rotary telephone hanging on the wall, connecting us with extended family and others in the surrounding area. Our old Philco radio informed us when Eisenhower won the election, and our new black-and-white Zenith TV brought Howdy Doody, Mighty Mouse, and The Lone Ranger into the living room.

Today, I find myself drawn to 1950s "collectible" items, especially for the kitchen. My nostalgia for these things can be traced directly to my grandmother. "Nonnie" told me I was her favorite of Mama's three girls, and she treated me like I was extra special. Because of my discreetly elevated status with Nonnie, visits to my grandparents' farm were always memorable occasions. I was allowed to explore the nooks and crannies of every room and look at all of Nonnie's pretty things. Just being there made me happy.

When I was born again at 26, one of the first things I did was write a letter to Nonnie, telling her I was "saved" and apologizing for being impatient with her when I was a teen. When I think of it now, I'm sure that letter brought tears to her eyes. Nonnie responded right away, expressing her excitement over my salvation, and of course, forgiving my poor behavior.

My grandmother was most certainly a Christian, and I always knew she loved me. Because of this love, I knew she had me covered in prayer.

Even in old age they will still produce fruit; they will remain vital and green - Psalm 92:14 NLT.

Yes, Nonnie "produced fruit" until the day she died at 95 years old. Even now, memories of her kindness and love are producing fruit in my heart—and her prayers are still being answered.

Lord, I thank you for all the memories of my grandmother. Your love through her was so sweet and special, and it certainly had an impact on my life. Thank You for all the special ones in our past who still reach us through our recollections of love.

Where is Your Comfort Zone?

December 2, 2015

We all want to be comfortable and content. It's simply human nature. Obtaining these things is a strong motivation for some and the *only* motivation for others.

Advertisers target our desire for physical and emotional fulfillment. If we will only buy what they offer, then we'll be happy, relaxed, satisfied and safe. We'll also smell good and look like supermodels. In time, we find these products delivering much less than promised. Some work temporarily, and others don't work at all. Sadly, we fall for many scams before we finally wise up.

Well then, if merchandise can't make us feel warm, comfy, and content, we'll have to take firm control of our personal world to keep discomfort at a distance. We'll erect a high wall of rules and order. We'll use our superior intellect to carve out a superior life—eating the right food, reading the right books, following the right leaders, and finding comfort in how exceedingly savvy we are. But to all of these good intentions, a day of reckoning comes.

In His great mercy, God lets the promise of commerce fail, and He pokes holes in the walls of our well-constructed forts. Then—He knocks on our doors and asks to come in.

Behold, I stand at the door and knock. If anyone hears My voice and opens the door, I will come in to him and dine with him, and he with Me - Revelation 3:20.

God doesn't need to advertise. He can always get our attention by pushing us out of our precarious self-made comfort zones. He doesn't mind putting us in difficult places that require us to reach for His hand.

Don't be surprised to hear the Lord say, "Choose ME to be your comfort zone. Come to ME to drink and dine. Before long, you'll find that I am your favorite place."

Lord, we're learning that comfort zones don't just appeal to the younger folks. ALL of us want the comfort that is only found in You.

God Will Complete His Work

February 19, 2016

In recent months, almost every time I meet with God, I begin thinking of His patience and longsuffering with me over the years. I love these attributes of God. I am *verrrry* thankful for His kindness in this area.

I often wonder why I've progressed so slowly. (At least it seems that way to me.) I look back on bright seasons of growth mixed with times of struggle, distraction, and failure. Over the years, I have pleaded with God to not give up on me, and I'm happy to say, He's answered that prayer. (I'm still living and breathing and *growing*.)

- When I've been apathetic, God has lit fires to wake me from my slumber. He's had to do this numerous times.

- When I've been selfish, God has lovingly showed me better ways. He's done this over and over, year after year.

- When I've been prideful or presumptuous, instead of angrily deflating my balloon, God has patiently shined His light on the error of my ways.

- When I've indulged in "little sins" like poor eating habits, watching something unGodly on TV, or reacting verbally when someone is unkind, the Lord has convicted me, but He's never condemned me.

I think you get the picture, and you can probably identify with what I've described. I know the Lord is longsuffering with all of us. He's determined to have His way in our hearts and in our lives, no matter how long it takes.

...He who has begun a good work in you will complete it until the day of Jesus Christ... - Philippians 1:6.

Thank You, Lord, for Your patience and longsuffering. Thank You for the amazing work You've begun in each of us. It's so good to know that You will finish Your work and also excel in it.

Let's Get Creative

January 30, 2016

Of all the crazy things, I've been photographing traffic as it moves on the interstate at night. It's really a lot of fun, and the creative possibilities are far-reaching. Of course, since God has been creative from the beginning of time, He passed this valuable attribute on to His children. We see proof of it throughout the world, in almost endless expression.

Some may think that human creativity is limited to things like photography, painting, or home decor. And if we're so inclined, we might reach farther to architecture, engineering, or a form of science to exhibit our ingenuity. All of these things are good, but God has even *more* for us. Instead of limiting us to physical materials for use in drawing, building, and even growing things, He invites us to a higher domain with a loftier purpose.

As born-again Christians, we have prime access to the creative, restorative power of God's written Word. Every verse is a building block. Every precept is a tool. Instead of settling for what we see around us, we can use the Word to bring much-needed change. First, we flip the power-switch of faith, then we ask the Holy Spirit to hand us the proper tool.

By proclaiming the Word, highways of truth and bridges of hope appear. By praying the Word, wounded hearts are healed, and broken homes are repaired. And by teaching the Word, life-giving light shines deep into the darkest night.

For we are His workmanship, created in Christ Jesus for good works, which God prepared beforehand that we should walk in them - Ephesians 2:10.

As the Bride of Christ, our time on Earth is practice for the work of eternity—for all that we'll do as co-heirs and co-rulers with our glorious Lord. Let's pick up the Word and use it to build something beautiful!

Oh, Lord, how can we ever express our thanks for Your generosity? We love opportunities that You have given us.

It's Only Gonna Get Better!

January 22, 2016

My soul shall make its boast in the LORD; the humble shall hear of it and be glad. Oh, magnify the LORD with me, and let us exalt His name together - Psalm 34:2-3.

When I get up early to spend time with the Lord in my prayer room, first I light one or more candles. (This is not a "religious" thing. I do it because meeting with God is *special*.) Then I open the mini-blinds so I can watch the dawn. I'm in a rural location, so I feel sure that no one is looking in at me.

On a recent morning, I was reading from my Bible, using a flashlight instead of a lamp, when I noticed red-orange light reflecting off the wall. I looked out the window and saw a spectacular sunrise. It seemed that God was saying, "*Good morning, Susan. Look out here, and see what I've made for you. You're going to like the color.*"

This only happened to me because I was in the right place at the right time—meeting with God, first thing in the morning. When I respond to His invitation, I'm never disappointed.

I'm finding that God *loves* to love me. He gives me very special personal gifts that are "homemade"—like a sunrise, a bird nest filled with eggs, or a phone call from a friend. He tells me the most exciting things, day after day after day. (With God, the good news never ends.) And He often tickles my funny bone. Sometimes I laugh out loud at the humorous thoughts we share.

I can't imagine not being this close to God. And now I'm smiling because I know for sure...*It's only gonna get better!*

Lord, we thank you for being with us 24 hours each day. You never leave us or forsake us (Deuteronomy 31:8), and Your presence will only get better as we come to know You more.

Paid in Full

January 14, 2016

O LORD God of hosts, who is mighty as you are, O LORD, with your faithfulness all around you? – Psalm 89:8 ESV.

For the past ten years, I've wondered how I would ever retire. My worst imagination was that I would work until I was so old that I would be asked to leave. I hoped that wouldn't be the case, and I looked to God for help. I leaned on His word for support, and I faithfully tithed. Then the day came when God directed me to retire. I was afraid to do it because of financial concerns, so I asked Him to give me courage. About a week later, my courage had grown tremendously, so I gave my notice.

And ever since I bought my house in 2001, I've expected to make payments until I sold it or died, whichever came first. But it was two weeks ago when God gave me a revelation: I could use my two modest retirement accounts to completely pay off my mortgage. Then my Social Security check would be adequate to pay my monthly bills. Today, I checked my online mortgage statement to see if the wire-transfer payment had been credited. I was thrilled to see the beautiful words on my computer screen, "PAID IN FULL!"

God is GOOD! He is very *very* good, and He is FAITHFUL!

Being free from financial debt is awesome, but having the debt for my sin paid in full by Jesus' precious blood is even better. People are sometimes unforgiving, but it's God's opinion of me that matters. It's His presence that gives me peace and His love that makes me whole. It is God's sweet words that warm my heart each day.

Dear Lord, please keep it coming. Let it be done to all of us according to Your word. Please continue to bless us so we can bless others.

____

____

____

One Prayer

December 27, 2015

How many of you remember reading The Prayer of Jabez, a small but important book that was published in 2000? This tiny volume got the attention of readers around the world. I was reminded of the prayer of Jabez again on Christmas morning when reading from a devotional book that mentions his prayer.

The name, Jabez, is only recorded in the following two verses of the Bible:

Now Jabez was more honorable than his brothers, and his mother called his name Jabez, saying, "Because I bore him in pain." And Jabez called on the God of Israel saying, "Oh, that You would bless me indeed, and enlarge my territory, that Your hand would be with me, and that You would keep me from evil, that I may not cause pain!" So God granted him what he requested - 1 Chronicles 4:9-10.

Fifteen years later, my only remembrance from the book about Jabez is that "God answers prayer." So when I read this scripture again, it was the Holy Spirit who spoke to me: *This one prayer was important enough to be included in the Bible.*

One prayer can be substantial. Not only did God answer Jabez' plea for help, He honored the man with a place of great significance. Jabez is now an example for us to follow.

Jabez prayed in faith, knowing that God wanted to bless him, accompany him, and deliver him from the curse of a name meaning "sorrow maker."

Let's begin the new year by asking God to prosper and enlarge us, to walk with us daily, to guide and protect us, and to make us a blessing to others instead of a stumbling block. We can pray with confidence, knowing that our Father wants to answer

Yes, Lord, please answer this prayer for us, just as You did for Jabez. We want to help others and not hurt them. We want to love and not hate.

One With God

October 28, 2015

One afternoon last week when I began my "quiet time" with God, I started off being rather chatty—just telling Him all sorts of things. I was not feeling at all quiet. Then the thought came to me that God and I are quite a mismatched pair, and I laughingly told Him so. I thought of God in His great big awesomeness and then of myself in my frail, goofy, needy humanness. For some reason, this really struck my funny bone. I laughed and laughed as I visualized the contrast. I think God saw the humor in this too. *But then I was made keenly aware that we are not a "pair."* God reminded me that we are ONE.

**He who is joined to the Lord is one spirit with Him –
1 Corinthians 6:17.**

How incredible it is to be *one spirit with God*—and to be reminded of it! Needless to say, *you* are one with God too, provided you're born again.

A lifetime here on Earth is not sufficient to fully explore this truth. But we can certainly start. *Just think of the potential!*

Lord, please don't let us miss out on any of Your goodness. Don't let us be so distracted by this world that we should forego the wonders of our connection with You.

____

____

____

____

____

____

____

PURPOSE

Redeem the Time

September 17, 2006

Time is running out. The sun is dropping low in the sky of this spiritual era. If we want to play a significant role in the grand finale, we must get our ducks in a row. Of course, these are "ducks of grace" and not of human works. The areas we've neglected must hold a new priority. Without the Word, we are foolish and weak. Without prayer, the victories we desire will not take place. Without worship, we can't enter God's presence and enjoy Him.

As for me, a sense of urgency has begun to permeate my days—a resolve to accomplish the will of God and a strong desire to please Him. Most of what I do is now measured against a plumb-line of spiritual accountability. With all of my time, I assess the eternal value.

I must work the works of Him who sent Me while it is day; the night is coming when no one can work - John 9:4.

A common demonic strategy is to sidetrack us from our purpose in these last days. We're attacked at our weakest points repeatedly with whatever it takes to extinguish our hope and derail us. We must recognize this evil plan, then quickly draw near to God for strength and strategy. In His glorious presence, we easily switch from defense to offense. Our fears are dissolved, and hope is reborn.

Therefore He says: "Awake, you who sleep, arise from the dead, and Christ will give you light." See then that you walk circumspectly, not as fools but as wise, redeeming the time, because the days are evil - Ephesians 5:14-16.

Dear Lord, You know how weak we are without You. Please keep us very close. Keep us wide awake to the peril around us—unafraid and walking in the authority and power You won for us on the cross. Let us not lose sight of the goals You've assigned to each of us.

In Position

November 2, 2006

The story of Joseph holds many lessons for Christians today. One of them is the importance of being in the right place at the right time—with the right attitude. Because Joseph bowed his spirit to the mighty Spirit of God, he was in perfect alignment with His providential plan.

After 13 years in captivity, Joseph's big breakthrough happened in the span of a few hours. One minute he was in jail, performing his daily chores. A short while later, he was clean-shaven and wearing his best prison clothes while standing before Pharaoh. Because Joseph drew near to God during his years of confinement, he was able to interpret Pharaoh's two dreams. Then he boldly and wisely advised him on how to prepare for the future. Before the sun set that day, Joseph was hearing these words from Pharaoh:

You shall be over my house, and all my people shall be ruled according to your word; only in regard to the throne will I be greater than you." And Pharaoh said to Joseph, "See, I have set you over all the land of Egypt." Then Pharaoh took his signet ring off his hand and put it on Joseph's hand; and he clothed him in garments of fine linen and put a gold chain around his neck. And he had him ride in the second chariot which he had; and they cried out before him, "Bow the knee!" So he set him over all the land of Egypt. Pharaoh also said to Joseph, "I am Pharaoh, and without your consent no man may lift his hand or foot in all the land of Egypt" - Genesis 41:40-44.

Talk about a promotion! Joseph went directly from imprisonment to second-in-command of Egypt.

God has a plan for each of His children, to use us in powerful ways. If we are submitted to Him and are waiting faithfully—in position—for as long as He requires, then our change of status will also come to pass. This may be gradual, or it could be quite dramatic. God will bless us with material goods, but more importantly, He will increase our influence in this world. Like Joseph, our words and actions will help many people.

And Joseph said to his brothers, "Please come near to me." So they came near. Then he said: "I am Joseph your brother, whom you sold into Egypt. But now, do not therefore be grieved or angry with yourselves because you sold me here; for God sent me before you to preserve life. For these two years the famine has been in the land, and there are still five years in which there will be neither plowing nor harvesting. And God sent me before you to preserve a posterity for you in the earth, and to save your lives by a great deliverance - Genesis 45:7.

Help us, Lord, to position ourselves within the realm of Your grace. (Let us never be caught in a trap of works.) Please give us a vision of Your plan for us. Not for ourselves, we ask these things, but to serve You and to bless Your people as life on Earth draws to a close.

Embrace Your Individuality

August 1, 2006

Most animals begin their lives in spring or summer, when the air is warm, and food is plentiful. Last week I found a nest of baby wrens inside my garage. The mother flies in through an open window with fresh bugs to drop into hungry mouths. These tiny creatures will fly from the nest at less than three weeks old. Earlier this summer, my sister found a newborn turtle in a creek near her home. To increase its chance of survival, she's keeping it in an aquarium for its first year.

Baby birds are tenderly cared for, needing only a few weeks before they fly and a couple more months to become mature. In contrast, turtles are abandoned at birth and will need many years to reach full size. Of course the purpose of birds is quite different from the purpose of turtles.

Like the animals, our place of birth and ongoing circumstances are designed by God to prepare us for a specific purpose in life. Some people are like baby birds, getting a quick jump off the starting line. And others are born into adversity, growing slowly but surely and overcoming great odds. They are very much like the turtle. Because God is perfectly sovereign and wise, every person's experience and rate of growth will line up with His plan for them.

...all things work together for good to those who love God, to those who are the called according to His purpose - Romans 8:28.

If you trust God completely with your life, there's no need to compare yourself with others. *Embrace your individuality!* You are distinctive and irreplaceable. Everything you've enjoyed or endured has brought you to a special place and is moving you deeper into your destiny.

Lord, if we're grounded in Your wonderful grace, then we can more easily trust Your action in our lives. Please remind us often that You have amazing plans to transform us and to use us in Your kingdom.

____

____

____

Discomfort Pushes Us Higher

April 5, 2007

When tiny birds become too large for the captivity of their shell, they peck their way out to the comfort of a spacious nest. A few weeks later, the new living quarters are crowded, so at the mother's urging, they fly to a nearby branch. The birds' territory gradually increases until they claim their own domain, several miles away. Christian growth is about the same. God doesn't save us and transform us, only to keep us hidden away in a small dark space. Certainly not! He is training us to *fly*.

Just as with the birds, discomfort bids us to break free and advance to a place that fits our maturing desires, needs, and goals. Uneasiness keeps us focused on the task of moving forward instead of becoming stagnant. And since we're spiritual creatures, we must use spiritual strength to claim the fullness of our destinies.

A friend of mine has some physical handicaps. God recently gave her a vivid dream in which she was running on a beach with no bodily limitations. At first my friend thought God was showing her a preview of heaven. But when the identical dream was repeated, she decided that God was offering her something new here on Earth. To prevent my friend from accepting her current situation, God gave her a taste of something better. He increased her desire to be free of her confinement, and now she prays for the healing she has seen.

Like a mother bird, God lures us from our tiny nests to increasingly higher branches. These changes can be difficult and frightening, but the purpose and joy of flying high are worth the effort.

But we all, with unveiled face, beholding as in a mirror the glory of the Lord, are being transformed into the same image from glory to glory, just as by the Spirit of the Lord - 2 Corinthians 3:18.

Thank You, Lord, for the "glory to glory" pace You have set for us. We're transformed in wonderful increments as we follow Your example.

God Has Chosen the Weak

August 1, 2008

The Lord goes to great lengths to strip away our pride and show us our need of Him. To accomplish this, He may choose to surround us with those who have more education and money, greater social skills, and superior physical attributes. It's good for us to have a realistic view of our human condition.

It's also important to see how the unsaved world operates when pursuing an agenda. Systems and fraternities exist to protect and promote their own. We are often considered dispensable if we get in someone's way. Against these groups, a Christian cannot stand without the help of God. So in addition to our weakness, we find that we live in a world of greedy, ruthless people.

However, with God, there is always good news:

**But God has chosen the foolish things of the world to put to shame the wise, and God has chosen the weak things of the world to put to shame the things which are mighty; and the base things of the world and the things which are despised God has chosen, and the things which are not, to bring to nothing the things that are, that no flesh should glory in His presence –
1 Corinthians 1:27-29.**

Now that's exciting! If you are weak or base or despised, then the Lord desires to use YOU to pull down some mighty strongholds. If you draw near to Him and align with His holy purpose, then through YOU the unsaved world will behold the power and love of God.

Lord, You are so good! First, You show us our weakness, then You use that same weakness as a vessel of Your strength. We are humbled and forever thankful.

____

____

____

Personal Missions

June 5, 2008

Every day we're confronted with the difficulties in this world. Many people are without food and shelter while others use vast resources to promote their evil agendas. Family values are under siege, and our children are pummeled with filth by the entertainment industry. Society crumbles around us as we watch.

What can we do to change these things? Where do we start? Can we even make a dent in the mountain of problems? What does God require from us? Let me offer some answers:

First of all, we must pray. We can stop disease, resolve conflicts and make our world much better by simply praying in faith. We dare not neglect this mighty weapon.

We need to give. Being led by the Spirit, we must give to individuals, churches, or Godly organizations. This action blesses us as well as others, especially when done with a joyful heart.

Our spiritual gifts should be exercised. If we are prophets, teachers, or healers, then we must use what God has given us. With these gifts, we offer life and hope to others.

We need to be available. Our Lord has marvelous plans to transform parts of this world through each of us. Since the day we were born, He's been grooming us for unique projects and ministry that are perfectly matched to our experience, gifts, and talents. We must listen for His calls to action.

Let's do it by grace. "Good works" are not an option. Whatever we do for the Lord, we must do by His grace. This essential gift de-stresses and empowers our action. We must walk in grace and pass it on to others.

Also I heard the voice of the LORD, saying: "Whom shall I send, and who will go for Us?" Then I said, "Here am I! Send me" – Isaiah 6:8.

Lord, send each one of us! Awaken our hearts to the need around us. Teach us how to proceed with Your work. We'll make no more excuses.

Through the Fire

April 13, 2016

Beloved, do not think it strange concerning the fiery trial which is to try you, as though some strange thing happened to you; but rejoice to the extent that you partake of Christ's sufferings, that when His glory is revealed, you may also be glad with exceeding joy – 1 Peter 4:12-13.

All of us are called to be tested, and many are called to be *greatly* tested. But we need not fear this aspect of Christian life because tests of our faith are always a blessing. If we turn to God for help, we're drawn deeper into His heart where we find much reason to rejoice.

> *Great faith is the product of great fights. Great testimonies are the outcome of great tests. Great triumphs can only come out of great trials. - Smith Wigglesworth*

Are *you* going through a fiery trial? Then, above all, know that you are not alone. The Lord is closer than ever before. His heart beats with intense love as He guides you through the flames. Sometimes the Lord will carry you, gently insisting that you *"Be still and know that I am God"* (Psalm 46:10).

Testing and trials come for numerous reasons. I was reading through Ephesians the other day when the Spirit showed me an outcome of our testing that I was previously unaware of—something interesting and remarkable:

[The purpose is] that through the church the complicated, many-sided wisdom of God in all its infinite variety and innumerable aspects might now be made known to the angelic rulers and authorities (principalities and powers) in the heavenly sphere – Ephesians 3:10 AMPC.

It seems that Heaven's holy angels are learning about God by observing us—by seeing the work of Jesus blossom and flourish in our lives. We know that angels fiercely stand guard over us and intervene with supernatural power on many occasions, but we don't think of them watching and learning. The thought of this warms my heart and encourages me more than ever to be "strong and of good courage" (Joshua 1:9), putting the Lord on display. If God is using Christians to teach His mighty angels, then who are we to complain about trials?

But most importantly, the frail members of fallen humanity are watching as we submit to God, letting His power, grace, and love manifest fully before their eyes. We only have to yield to the Lord's great choreography, saying "Yes" at every turn. By His amazing grace, we will march and even dance through the fire.

Lord, we thank You for giving us work that has eternal significance. Thank You for the excitement and hope You inspire during these last days. We depend completely on Your faithfulness, mercy, and grace.

Share the Grace

August 18, 2009

Is this not the fast that I have chosen: To loose the bonds of wickedness, to undo the heavy burdens, to let the oppressed go free, and that you break every yoke? Is it not to share your bread with the hungry, and that you bring to your house the poor who are cast out; when you see the naked, that you cover him, and not hide yourself from your own flesh? - Isaiah 58:6-7.

Our hearts should never become immune to the pain we see around us. We find people who are poor, hungry, dirty, lonely, and totally without God. We must take time to help and encourage them—to share the grace that we've been given.

When God tells us to give to the poor and oppressed, He's speaking of more than money. We all have time, gifts, and talents to offer. If we know the Lord, then certainly we have wisdom to share. Some Christians are gifted with encouragement, and others are wonderful teachers. I know people who are great with children and others who have compassion for the elderly. Developing relationships and helping others to walk in victory with the Lord is worth every bit of the effort.

Lord, please don't let us be self-obsessed. Help us trust You with meeting our needs while we invest our time in others.

As to the Lord

May 8, 2009

Work willingly at whatever you do, as though you were working for the Lord rather than for people. Remember that the Lord will give you an inheritance as your reward, and that the Master you are serving is Christ - Colossians 3:23-24 NLT.

Try to imagine turning every facet of your life over to the Lord—submitting all thoughts, words and actions to Him. Everything would be used to bless the heart of God and to serve His holy purpose.

Working, playing, and "doing all" for the Lord would eliminate many temptations that come with doing these things for men. Manipulation would quickly lose its allure. Self-serving competition would be totally out of place. Fear of losing man's favor would vanish. All of your energy could now be spent on works of the kingdom. Pleasing God would be of utmost importance.

And of course, none of what you do "as to the Lord" would ever be unappreciated. Because God sees, hears, and knows all things, then He gives every prize and compensation with full knowledge, perfect love, and plenty of His amazing grace.

Dear Lord, please help us submit to You in every area of life.

 Over Fifty?

May 28, 2009

Are you over fifty? Over sixty or seventy? Are you serious about the kingdom of God? If so, I'm sure you've heard discouraging words from Satan's camp: "Time has run out. Your life has been wasted. There's no use trying to be a victorious Christian at *your* age." The attack goes on and on: "You're a big disappointment to God. He had high hopes for you, but after all these years, He's finally given up."

But, as you've probably heard, Satan only tries to discourage us if we're a genuine threat. The enemy doesn't want us aware of how mature and wise we've probably become. The worse we feel about ourselves, the better off is the kingdom of darkness. It's important to remember that our success is measured by God, and He values things that we might overlook. For example, the quality of no longer being offended by careless remarks may not be something we're aware of, but it will probably be circled and highlighted by God. I imagine Him being excited every time we "get it right."

Now let's take a look at Moses. He spent more than fifty years in the little town of Midian, from early adulthood until he was about eighty. During this time, Satan surely tormented him with endless "what ifs" as he quietly tended his sheep. "What if you hadn't killed that Egyptian?" "What if you had used your influence and patiently worked for change within the system?" Maybe Moses thought he had blown his chance to help God's people. But instead, for all of his life so far, Moses was being carefully trained for the important years ahead.

We don't know the details of Moses' training in Midian, but we do know the results. At eighty years old, he was physically strong and spiritually mature. We also know he was humble: On the day God spoke from a burning bush, Moses was personally tending flocks on the back side of the desert instead of resting while a younger man did the job.

...there has not arisen in Israel a prophet like Moses, whom the LORD knew face to face, in all the signs and wonders which the LORD sent him to do in the land of Egypt, before Pharaoh, before all his servants, and in all his land, and by all that mighty power

and all the great terror which Moses performed in the sight of all Israel - Deuteronomy 34:10-12.

So, to every one of you who is over fifty and feeling insignificant in the kingdom; understand that you are still in training. You may be tending some of the stinkiest sheep in the world. Or maybe you're lonely and feeling forgotten on the back side of somewhere you dislike. But if you continue to humble yourself and submit to God, then He will surely exalt you according to His plan.

Dear Lord, the ones of us who are over fifty are beginning to appreciate the wisdom and insight gained through the years—everything we've learned, whether through obedience or as a consequence. Thank You for Your patience and longsuffering. Please Lord, do not let us fail at whatever You have planned.

God's Perspective

August 3, 2010

We often get bogged down in the negative aspects of our circumstances and relationships. One of the enemy's favorite lies is that "things will never change." It's important to remember that the length of our days on Earth are just a drop in the bucket compared to eternity—but the *impact* of that short time will be known forever. Instead of fretting about our difficulties, we must turn our entire being to the Lord and to His purpose. When we do that, all fear and discouragement will flee from the light of His grace toward us.

When people don't love us like they should, it helps to think of how God is loving each of us, every minute of every day. You and I are adored by Him. He wants the very best for us, even if it requires our distress for a little while. We can consider these times of suffering as opportunities to pray for others.

So be truly glad. There is wonderful joy ahead, even though you must endure many trials for a little while. These trials will show that your faith is genuine. It is being tested as fire tests and purifies gold—though your faith is far more precious than mere gold. So when your faith remains strong through many trials, it will bring you much praise and glory and honor on the day when Jesus Christ is revealed to the whole world – 1 Peter 1:6-7 NLT.

Today may bring loneliness to some. If that includes you, then try spending some of the hours conversing with God. Acknowledge His presence in the room, and speak to Him throughout the day, wherever you go and whatever you do. The enemy will whisper depressing lies about your loneliness lasting forever, but you can always combat this with truth. Meanwhile, your Best Friend will answer your prayers for human friends and the restoration of family.

As we develop an intimate friendship with the Lord, He will speak to us about all that is important, whether it be relationships, health, ministry, or financial matters. By giving us truth and understanding, He is giving us His perspective. God's holy thoughts will be ours. His truth will light our paths and guide our steps. His love will warm our hearts and replace every Earthly concern with the transforming power of peace and joy.

How precious also are Your thoughts to me, O God! How great is the sum of them! - Psalm 139:17.

Thank You for Your friendship, Lord, and for Your holy perspective. You take us "outside the box" of human thinking, and that's a wonderful thing.

According to His Purpose

March 1, 2011

And we know that all things work together for good to those who love God, to those who are the called according to His purpose. For whom He foreknew, He also predestined to be conformed to the image of His Son, that He might be the firstborn among many brethren - Romans 8:28-29.

God's number one purpose for Christians is that we be conformed to His image. The number one purpose of our flesh is to get what it wants and be happy. These two objectives often collide. Our flesh doesn't think and feel on the same level that God does. When abiding in Christ, our spirits are wonderfully meshed with His, but our flesh remains weak and self-centered (Matthew 26:41).

Every Christian is caught in this primary conflict between God's intention and the desires of their fleshly human nature. Identifying and being aware of this conflict is helpful. It's good to know what may be slowing down our spiritual progress.

Submitting to God isn't easy, but the Spirit always shines His light for us to step forward in the process. He reminds us that "all things" are working together for our good if we are born again and belong to Him. Revelation of God's sovereignty and goodness will ease our distress when we're feeling emotional conflict with His purpose. Believing in God's love for us will decrease our fear of feeling trapped or "losing control."

Let me offer an example: If you want to tame a feral cat, you begin with setting out food and water. You talk to the wild animal with a soothing voice, never making sudden moves. Gaining the cat's trust takes weeks or months. You want to touch it, bring it into your home, and eventually take it to the vet for protection from parasites and disease. Your goal is to have a healthy, contented cat that is safe from harm and able to receive your love. *This process is a good reflection of how God deals with us.*

The Lord moves slowly but always with purpose. He knows we don't understand His higher ways, so He offers us His Spirit and His Word.

When we get comfortable with a new level of trust in Him, then He calls for a little more. During each experience with God, we learn that He is truly good. Whenever we respond to Him by moving closer, we're rewarded by an increase of His blessing and His presence.

Lord, we thank You for giving us Your best, in spite of our fearful resistance. Thank You for the enlightenment of Your Word and Your Spirit. We praise You for Your patience, Your mercy, and Your most amazing grace!

The Safest Place to Be

All Christians have to go through tests and trials. These difficult times are a part of our training for the work that eternity holds. Tribulation is not optional. We can't claim exemption for any reason.

Testing is a vehicle that transports our spiritual theology to the place of glorious reality.

Amidst the challenge of a test, we're given a chance to show the world who God really is—to show the lost what He will do when we trust in Him. Times of tribulation are true contests between good and evil, with *much* riding on the outcome. Fear will come from all directions to undermine our faith, but the light of God's Word brings power and peace in abundance.

Do not be afraid; only believe – Mark 5:36.

As we mature, the tests we encounter will increase in difficulty, so don't be surprised when the enemy "comes out swinging." Some days may seem darker than a cloudy night. Seas may rise up with towering waves that threaten to overwhelm us. But God is *Love*, and a test has only come our way because He will carry us through it—if we listen to Him. The enemy plans for us to fail, but God always sets us up for victory. Satan may be saying, "Check!" But if we submit to God in faith, He will always say, "Check Mate!"

Any serious trial will directly target our faith: Do we really believe what God has said? Is He faithful to keep His words? We may know a lot *about* God, but do we actually know *Him*? We certainly can't trust someone we don't have experience with. A test will bring these things to light and open a door to connect with God more personally. And if we already have a close relationship, the test will stretch our faith to reach new heights.

Intimacy with God is the safety in any storm. Amidst the raging wind and crashing waves, He will speak loving, encouraging truth. He might remind us of a vision He's given for a time in the future. If we have a personal promise for tomorrow, then total disaster is *not* imminent. (If you don't have a view of your future provided by God, then now is the time to ask.)

Write the vision and make it plain on tablets, that he may run who reads it. For the vision is yet for an appointed time... – Habakkuk 2:2-3.

Knowing the faithfulness of God will carry us through any tempest. Recognizing the voice of our Shepherd will guide us to peace and rest.

For the LORD of hosts has purposed, and who will annul it? His hand is stretched out, and who will turn it back? – Isaiah 14:27.

God is the Alpha and the Omega. From beginning to end, He is the One whose purpose prevails. Sitting by His side is always the safest place to be (Ephesians 2:6).

Dear Lord and Master, Adonai, we thank You for Your extreme love. You go to great lengths, pulling out all the stops, to save the lost and perishing. Sometimes we find that tribulations are designed for more than our own training. Situations that discipline and enlighten us may also be saving another from the flames of hell. Your sovereignty is astounding, and Your love is beyond measure. Thank You for always being near

____ _______

____

____

____

____

____

____

____

Speak Life, Not Death

February 10, 2017

Christians are called to speak creative words of life into our personal domains. We should always be voicing positive, uplifting words over our family, friends, associates, church, town, state, country, and even distant lands as inspired by the Spirit.

To consistently speak negative, critical words is contrary to God's will. Those who insist on spewing their harsh judgments are in rebellion, and scripture calls this witchcraft. Refusing to speak life by giving someone the silent treatment is also rebellion and therefore witchcraft.

For rebellion is as the sin of witchcraft, and stubbornness is as iniquity and idolatry - 1 Samuel 15:23.

We are made in the image of God, and we should behave as such. In my experience, the Lord has been my biggest fan and my most devoted cheerleader. He's put in my heart the strong desire to encourage others. (Therefore, the times when I speak negatively, I feel just awful.)

What about you? Which path of influence will you walk upon? Will your tongue inspire and establish new life, or will it destroy the fragile growth around you?

Death and life are in the power of the tongue, and those who love it will eat its fruit – Proverbs 18:21.

Lord, we thank You for this powerful tongue You've given to us. Let it work for Your good. Let it always speak beautiful life.

Do Good

October 15, 2010

Therefore, to him who knows to do good and does not do it, to him it is sin – James 4:17.

We're required to do good, and because God is a giver and a helper, we should do the same. So then, should we give to everyone who asks? Certainly not. Should we help every person who is needy? No, we don't have the time. We are told to be good stewards of our resources, whether that is money, time, or energy. Being a good steward includes "not throwing pearls to swine" (Matthew 7:6). So how do we choose which people to help? Where do we sow our seed?

Having a close relationship with the Lord means we communicate with Him about many things, including our choices of action. If we're abiding in Him, we'll hear His voice when He prompts us to help someone. His heart will beat faster within us, and His Spirit will compel us to act. These are the calls to which we must respond.

For all who are led by the Spirit of God are children of God – Romans 8:14 NLT.

Many requests from God are for quick and simple acts of kindness. What may only take a few minutes of our time can alter the course of another's life. I feel honored when God uses me to meet a person's need. Because He's given me the gift of encouragement, He sends people to me who need uplifting words of truth.

We've all been given spiritual gifts that are meant to do good for others, but God is not limited by this. Opportunities come to us in numerous ways, requiring a variety of responses, sometimes outside our field of gifting. We shouldn't say "no" because we don't have a particular gift. Neither should we say "yes" just because we have the gift. We really do need to hear from God and use our time wisely. And, if we respond when the Spirit calls, occasions for doing good will continue to come our way.

Lord, please continue teaching us Your ways of holiness. Impart to us the arts of mercy and grace toward others, along with Your wisdom and discernment. Keep us always fully armed to do Your work.

COMMITMENT

The Time of Reckoning

November 29, 2006

Many who call themselves Christians are not really born again. They haven't reached that point of decision—the time of reckoning when they understand the level of commitment God requires from His people. Some get this revelation right away, while others need to travel down the road awhile before their eyes are completely opened.

I was slow to respond, even after attending church. At the time, I thought I was saved, and maybe I was. But I needed to understand my true condition before I was able to fully repent. I'm grateful that God deals with us individually. I want every reader to be aware that ultimately, the Lord insists on commitment.

So then, because you are lukewarm, and neither cold nor hot, I will vomit you out of My mouth - Revelation 3:16.

This world is a battleground, and God is recruiting soldiers. Christianity has never been a game.

Jesus' blood covers every one of our messy mistakes and wipes our slate clean every day—but only after we've come to the place of true remorse for our sin—only when we must have God above all else and lay our lives down in surrender to Him.

Not everyone who says to Me, "Lord, Lord," shall enter the kingdom of heaven, but he who does the will of My Father in heaven – Matthew 7:21.

Thank You, Lord, for not letting us sit on the fence. Thanks for not allowing us to play games. We truly thank You for Your patience and mercy. They're exactly what we need.

Only One Chance

May 13, 2006

We only have one life to live in our human bodies—only one life to honor God by fulfilling our destiny here on Earth. Will you rise to this glorious challenge? The end-time harvest has already begun. Millions are being saved, and miracles are increasing. If you want to be involved, it's time to turn the dial on your commitment meter up to high. All of heaven is watching to see if you'll do what the Lord is asking:

Therefore we also, since we are surrounded by so great a cloud of witnesses, let us lay aside every weight, and the sin which so easily ensnares us, and let us run with endurance the race that is set before us... - Hebrews 12:1.

It's certainly time to stop playing around. Do you understand the importance of spending time with God? Do you know that reading His Word, sitting quietly in His presence and praising Him throughout the day connects you to His heart and His power?

- Are you ready to experience more of God? Do you long to feel His presence and maybe hear His audible voice?

- Can you imagine laying hands on the sick and restoring them to perfect health? Do you see their joyful tears as they rise from their bed and walk?

- Do you see yourself teaching those who hunger for God? Inspired words coming from your mouth can turn a life around!

God is waiting to release His power to *you*. He wants to work His miracles through *you*. But for this to happen, your priorities must be in order. You must sacrifice your right to all that you think is yours. God must be your first priority—far ahead of television, the internet and personal fulfillment.

Does this sound radical? Yes, maybe. But "radical" is what God wants. He never insists on anything, but He will ask for everything.

I beseech you therefore, brethren, by the mercies of God, that you present your bodies a living sacrifice, holy, acceptable to God, which is your reasonable service. And do not be conformed to this world, but be transformed by the renewing of your mind, that you may prove what is that good and acceptable and perfect will of God – Romans 12:1-2.

Dear Lord, please fill us with passion to know You in a close, personal way. Let us know what stirs Your heart. Let us know what You plan for our destiny. We want to be set us on fire to fulfill Your plans.

____

____

____

____

____

____

____

____

____

____

____

____

____

Under the Mighty Hand of God

February 28, 2015

...the Son of Man did not come to be served, but to serve, and to give His life a ransom for many – Mark 10:45.

The Creator of Heaven and Earth, came into this sinful world to do the Father's will—to serve and to die. The same is required of me and you. Maybe we learned all this in the first few weeks of "Christianity 101." But did we understand it? Did we take the teaching seriously, or was it "seed sown among thorns," choked out by the cares of this world?

Can we think of ourselves as "good Christians" who are spiritually mature if we have little desire to pour out our life like Jesus did?

Most assuredly, I say to you, unless a grain of wheat falls into the ground and dies, it remains alone; but if it dies, it produces much grain – John 12:24.

I must admit that I recoil from completely and absolutely giving my life. Maybe to God, on a good day, but not to sinful humans. I want to retain some control over what I give and where I go. Fortunately, God only asks that I submit to Him, even though at times it may appear that I'm submitting to people.

Whenever the Spirit reminds me of my reluctance to "surrender all," I do my best to repent. I ask Him to change my heart, and then I always add, "...but please be gentle." Even as I tremble over the things that God may ask of me, I know that He is good—every minute of every day. He's proven this over and over. I have learned to trust Him, whether He's gentle or not.

The Lord has been busy transforming me, and I expect it to continue. His efforts with each of us will triumph over our stubborn flesh. And since He is faithful to finish what He has begun (Philippians 1:6), we needn't worry about Him throwing His hands up in frustration.

We are all being captured and changed by the Lord's goodness—utterly and eternally. The Living Word reaches out to us with love and hope and healing power.   He continually enlarges us, making more room for the Spirit to stretch out and be God. By His grace, we're learning to give our lives as a ransom for others—one day at a time—one hour at a time.

As we humble ourselves beneath the hand of God, the presence of Christ within us will rise and prevail. When people look into our eyes, the Spirit of God will be looking back at them.

Dear Lord, we thank You for Your relentless work on our behalf. We're glad you don't give up on us. Thank You for revealing Your heart to us, making it easier for us to "fall into the ground and die." Lord Jesus, we thank You for being our Example and our Enabler. We thank You for dying. But most of all, we thank You for LIVING.

When a Vision Tarries

May 18, 2006

Don't be discouraged if your vision from God has not yet materialized, even if ten years have passed. Please do not give up. Whatever the Lord has told you to do, no matter how big or seemingly small—just keep on doing it!

Noah worked on the ark for a long time. Bible scholars estimate that somewhere from 70 to 120 years passed between God's instructions for building the ark and when the flood began.

Joseph dreamed that all of his brothers along with "the sun, the moon and the eleven stars" would bow down to him. At least thirteen years went by while Joseph honed his management skills—first as a household slave and then as a prisoner. Finally, the day arrived when he was promoted to second-in-command over all of Egypt.

In God's appointed time, each of our destinies will unfold. We must be patient and not rush ahead with our own schedules and bright ideas. Sometimes our faith may waiver, but as we persevere with obedience, our roots will grow deep to strengthen our hold on the glory that lies ahead.

For the vision is yet for an appointed time; but at the end it will speak, and it will not lie. Though it tarries, wait for it; because it will surely come, it will not tarry - Habakkuk 2:3.

Visions are precious gifts that help to lead us forward. Thank You, Lord, for these personal views of our place in the future. Until You bring them to pass, please encourage us to know that they will "surely come."

Redeeming The Time

December 13, 2007

December is the busiest month of the year for most of us. The demands on our time and energy increase because of how we celebrate Christmas. We're easily pulled into the social and commercial vortex of this world if we don't exercise our power of choice.

You probably vow every year to do things differently next time. The truth is, we *can* make a difference in our Christmas celebration. If we "choose correctly" every day throughout the year, then our resolve will be strengthened when tackling December 25th—or whatever day we believe is Jesus' birthday. Spending more time with the Lord each day will increase our desire to properly celebrate His coming to Earth as a human child.

And whatever you do, do it heartily, as to the Lord and not to men... – Colossians 3:23.

Time is a precious commodity, especially in the hands of a Christian. By spending it wisely we will increase God's influence in this world. By choosing fellowship with the Lord instead of following worldly tradition, we will open wide many spiritual doors. More of God's blessing and power will flow into our lives and thereby into the world.

Therefore He says: "Awake, you who sleep, arise from the dead, and Christ will give you light." See then that you walk circumspectly, not as fools but as wise, redeeming the time, because the days are evil. Therefore do not be unwise, but understand what the will of the Lord is - Ephesians 5:14-17.

Lord, please make us increasingly aware of how little time we have left on Earth. Teach us to act only in accordance with Your will. Let us always seek to please You instead of ourselves.

Obedience Brings Confidence

God yearns for our affections, and He wants to have first place in our lives. But every time we disobey one of His principles or commands, we demote Him to second place. We may try to rationalize our sin, but this defensive ploy is born of the flesh and won't protect us from reaping negative consequences.

Self-exalting pride puts distance between us and the Lord. Evil spirits will whisper that "God is very unhappy with you" and "Now He won't answer your prayers." This distortion of truth is always used to condemn us—to isolate and destroy us. (God never stops loving us, and He will answer our prayers when we repent of the sin.)

On the positive side of this coin, obedience brings confidence. It delivers the fundamental reward of the principle followed, and it strengthens our relationship with the Lord.

God's mercy endures forever (Psalm 118:29). He is also longsuffering (Psalm 86:15). He sees the condition of our hearts, and He interacts with us using great compassion. God truly is on our side and goes to great lengths to help us eventually succeed. But, we should not take advantage of His love or test it too far. That would surely be asking for trouble. But if we do, God will respond in love with corrective measures.

And finally, obedience should never be confused with legalism. Christians are given plenty of grace and freedom, but when we *know* that God has given a command, obedience is always the perfect choice.

Now therefore, if you will indeed obey My voice and keep My covenant, then you shall be a special treasure to Me above all people; for all the earth is Mine. And you shall be to Me a kingdom of priests and a holy nation - Exodus 19:5-6.

Thank You so much, Lord, for giving us the choice to obey. Choosing wisely gets easier as time goes by because of You transforming us.

Seeking the Presence of God

February 9, 2007

Who may ascend into the hill of the LORD? Or who may stand in His holy place? He who has clean hands and a pure heart, who has not lifted up his soul to an idol, nor sworn deceitfully. He shall receive blessing from the LORD, and righteousness from the God of his salvation – Psalm 24:3-5.

Whoever wants to "ascend into the hill of the Lord," please raise your hand. Now, whoever will submit to all of God's requirements, keep your hand in the air. *Hmmm.* Is your hand still raised? Yes, I know that submitting to God can be difficult.   It means giving up our own control and trusting completely in His care for us.

What is the Holy Spirit asking of you? What do you need to let go of? Whatever stands between you and God for very long must be considered an idol to which you are "lifting up your soul." You might as well set a large golden calf on your dining room table.

You know that God is always good and wants you moving higher; climbing the hill into His presence. However, the enemy keeps increasing the efforts of every seduction.   Satan is afraid of what will happen when you reach the top of that hill—of what will transpire when you come face to face with God.

When You said, "Seek My face," my heart said to You, "Your face, LORD, I will seek" - Psalms 27:8.

Dear Lord, we thank You for Your patience. We're weak and frail, and we move very slowly. We need your mercy, but we especially need Your grace. Please let Your grace crash down upon us and flow through us, washing away all waywardness within. Let Your grace cause our hearts to be stronger, beating primarily for You.

July 27, 2010

There comes a time for every Christian when God points us toward a major life assignment. At first the details may be fuzzy, but that's okay. Training and preparation will keep us busy while waiting for sharper instructions to arrive.

The most important part of waiting is staying focused on the Lord while He teaches and tests. This sounds like a no-brainer, but life has a way of distracting us. Most of us would love to retrieve the time we've wasted on wrong turns and wild goose chases. God is merciful and patient when dealing with His children, but we must not push Him too far. Time is a valuable gift, and we are its stewards.

See then that you walk circumspectly, not as fools but as wise, redeeming the time, because the days are evil. Therefore do not be unwise, but understand what the will of the Lord is - Eph. 5:15-17.

Let's give our whole heart to God—never neglecting His assignments or ignoring His direction—always seeking His face and worshiping Him. *Nothing is more important.*

Not that I have already attained, or am already perfected; but I press on, that I may lay hold of that for which Christ Jesus has also laid hold of me. Brethren, I do not count myself to have apprehended; but one thing I do, forgetting those things which are behind and reaching forward to those things which are ahead, I press toward the goal for the prize of the upward call of God in Christ Jesus - Philippians 3:12-14.

We thank You, Lord, for our assignments from You. Especially the big ones. They keep us moving forward, out of the places we may have been stuck. Your work is always good work, and we are grateful for it.

____

____

____

Strip Off Every Weight

March 16, 2009

Therefore, since we are surrounded by such a huge crowd of witnesses to the life of faith, let us strip off every weight that slows us down, especially the sin that so easily trips us up. And let us run with endurance the race God has set before us. We do this by keeping our eyes on Jesus... – Hebrews 12:1-2 NLT.

While sin increases here on Earth, so does the silent cry for help from many anxious hearts. Enormous fields are ripe for harvest. A hunger for God is growing in these who belong to the Lord—in these who the Father has given to His Son. Every born-again saint should be focused on this waiting crop of souls. God has a role for each of us to play, and we must be in training.

Whether we have only a few hours or several decades remaining before the rapture comes, let's begin to "strip off every weight" that hinders us from running our race.   Whether we carry evangelism, teaching, prophecy, healing, or something else important, we must *run* with it.

The Holy Spirit will help us trim away all activities that rob us of His presence and His power. He will direct our hearts and minds to what is truly of value, enabling us to stay on this path. Deep joy and satisfaction will come with our activity in the Kingdom.

We're counting on You to strip off the weights that encumber us, Lord. Let Your passionate love through us be felt as a healing balm amidst the thorns. As we work, let our voices be heard in this noisy world.

Choosing God

January 24, 2008

Our thoughts and emotions don't always line up with God's perspective. A huge factor in our Christian growth is learning to get still, quiet, and in touch with the Lord. Once we're connected, we receive revelation that helps us align with His heart and purpose.

Getting "still, quiet, in touch, and aligned" takes time and determination. But as we allow Him, the Holy Spirit draws us near and helps us abide in God's presence. When we choose time with the Lord instead of a favorite activity, we are blessed in numerous ways. This spiritual momentum continues as long as we choose correctly.

"God resists the proud, but gives grace to the humble." Therefore submit to God. Resist the devil and he will flee from you. Draw near to God and He will draw near to you. Cleanse your hands, you sinners; and purify your hearts, you double-minded - James 4:6.

Scripture is crystal clear on the subject. God cares how we spend our time and energy. He wants us to pursue Him and His kingdom instead of the things in this world. I believe we can have as much of the Lord as we really want, so let's begin choosing Him in every hour of every day.

Lord, we thank You for choosing us and allowing us to draw near. Thank You for the love, peace, and bounty of revelation that we receive.

____

____

____

____

____

____

____

To God Be the Glory

I thank You, Lord, with all my heart, for the assignment and the grace to write this book. Thank You for always sitting by my side.

Please touch every reader in the ways You choose, and prepare them for the days to come. Let them be encouraged by reading these words, just as I was encouraged by writing them.

Thank You for Your perfect love.

All praise and honor and glory are Yours forever!